teen's
guides

LIVING
with
STRESS

Also in the
Teen's Guides series

Living with Alcoholism and Drug Addiction
Living with Allergies
Living with Anxiety Disorders
Living with Asthma
Living with Cancer
Living with Diabetes
Living with Depression
Living with Eating Disorders
Living with the Internet and Online Dangers
Living with Obesity
Living with Peer Pressure and Bullying
Living with Sexually Transmitted Diseases
Living with Skin Conditions
Living with Sports Injuries

teen's guides

LIVING
with
STRESS

Allen R. Miller, Ph.D.
with Susan Shelly

Checkmark Books®
An imprint of Infobase Publishing

Living with Stress

Checkmark Books
An imprint of Facts On File, Inc.
132 West 31st Street
New York NY 10001

Library of Congress Cataloging-in-Publication Data

Miller, Allen R.
  Living with stress / by Allen R. Miller with Susan Shelly.
    p. cm. — (Teen's guides)
  Includes bibliographical references and index.
  ISBN-13: 978-0-8160-7887-5 (hardcover : alk. paper)
  ISBN-10: 0-8160-7887-4 (hardcover : alk. paper)
  ISBN-13: 978-0-8160-7888-2 (pbk. : alk. paper)
  ISBN-10: 0-8160-7888-2 (pbk. : alk. paper) 1. Stress management—Popular works. 2. Stress in adolescence—Popular works. I. Shelly, Susan. II. Title.

  RA785.M525 2010
  616.9'8—dc22   2009032843

Checkmark Books are available at special discounts when purchased in bulk quantities for businesses, associations, institutions or sales promotions. Please call our Special Sales Department in New York at (212) 967-8800 or (800) 322-8755.

You can find Facts On File on the World Wide Web at http://www.factsonfile.com

Excerpts included herewith have been reprinted by permission of the copyright holders; the author has made every effort to contact copyright holders. The publishers will be glad to rectify, in future editions, any errors or omissions brought to their notice.

Text design by Annie O'Donnell
Composition by Hermitage Publishing Services
Cover printed by Art Print, Taylor, Pa.
Book printed and bound by Maple-Vail Book Manufacturing Group, York, Pa.
Date printed: June 2010
Printed in the United States of America

10 9 8 7 6 5 4 3 2 1

This book is printed on acid-free paper.

CONTENTS

1 What Is Stress? 1

2 What Causes Stress? 9

3 Why Teens Are at Risk for Stress-Related Problems 19

4 How Stress Affects You Physically 32

5 How Stress Affects You Emotionally 41

6 Long-term Physical Effects of Stress 50

7 Long-term Psychological Effects of Stress 62

8 Addressing Your Stress Problem with Lifestyle Changes 72

9 When Lifestyle Changes Aren't Enough 92

10 Helping Others Deal with Stress 110

11 Paying for Care 120

Appendix: Associations and Resources Related to Stress 129

Glossary 140

Read More About It 146

Index 149

What Is Stress?

Sometimes Lara likes to just sit and remember what life was like when she was a kid instead of a 16-year-old high school junior. She remembers riding her bike in her neighborhood and spending time with an older couple who lived next door. Her mom and dad used to take her to the movies or to visit her cousins, or she and her mom and brother would go on camping trips with her mom's friends and their kids.

These days, though, Lara's mom is too busy working and going to meetings to talk to her, and Lara would rather be with her friends anyway, at least when they're all getting along and somebody isn't spreading lies on Facebook about somebody else.

Lara is also worried about her grades this year, because she needs a scholarship to go to college, given that there's a chance her dad could lose his job. And then what would she do? Live at home with her parents while her friends go off to college?

Plus, something happened with her dad's medicine recently and his diabetes got really bad; he had to be in the hospital over the holiday season. He seems to be okay, but Lara is always afraid that something else is going to happen to him. Sometimes Lara wishes more than anything that she was little again.

Lara, like many other teens, is experiencing a lot of stress on different levels. She worries about her father's health and whether he'll be able to keep his job, and she feels resentful that her mother doesn't have more time to spend with her. She enjoys hanging out with her friends, but she doesn't like that they sometimes fight and are mean to one another. And she worries about her grades, afraid that her entire future depends on what happens in school this year.

That's a lot of stress for anyone to handle, and Lara is not alone. A recent study at the University of Michigan in Ann Arbor revealed that one-third of teens report feeling stressed out on a daily basis, and two thirds feeling stressed at least once a week. Most of us hear a lot about stress. Like Lara, you and your friends probably say things like "I am so stressed out about this paper I have to write," or "I had a really stressful situation with my boyfriend last weekend." You might hear your parents talk about being stressed over their financial situation or because the car isn't working right. Even children can experience stress when they don't get what they want or their lives are disrupted in some way. The Internet, magazines, and newspapers are loaded with articles about stress, and advertisements for products that claim to relieve stress. But what is stress, really?

Stress is how your body responds to pressure caused by a particular situation, such as a test, that requires you to adjust or respond. *Stress* can refer both to the stimulus that causes you to react—such as the test—and to your reaction to that stimulus. For example, if you feel yourself getting anxious and nervous about a test you have this afternoon, the test is a *stressor*—a situation that is leading you to feel a particular way. Your reaction to the test you have this afternoon also can be thought of as stress. You are worried about the test, and you're exhibiting stress by feeling anxious and nervous.

When someone asks you what stress means to you, you might think about term papers, peer pressure, teasing in school, relationship issues, parents, a younger brother or sister, and a number of other things. Everyone experiences stress, and stress is not necessarily a bad thing. If you didn't feel a degree of stress regarding the test, you might be inclined to just sit around and watch TV rather than study for it. If getting into a fight with your mom didn't cause you to feel stress, you probably wouldn't care so much about your relationship with her.

It's normal to feel stress. In fact, in our fast-paced society, where many people feel they're expected to achieve well in academics, financial and social standings, family and other relationships, careers, and so forth, it's practically impossible *not* to feel stress.

GOOD STRESS AND BAD STRESS

Good stress may sound like an oxymoron, but it's true that a small amount of stress can actually be a positive thing. Did you ever perform in the school play, or run the 100-meter race during a really close track event against your school's top rival? How about standing up in

Stressed? You Are Not Alone

It's important to remember that when you feel stressed about something, you're not alone. The majority of teens, at least on occasion, experience stress related to school, society, family, and peers. Teenagers are notoriously hard on themselves, worrying that they won't fit in; they won't succeed in school; they'll never get a boyfriend/girlfriend; they won't have the right clothes, or hair, or house; their friends won't like them anymore. The list goes on and on. All of these issues, and many others, can cause intense feelings of stress. Knowing that others your age are feeling stressed about exactly the same sorts of issues that you are might not make you feel less stressed, but at least you know you're in good company.

front of the class to present your book report, or waiting to hear back whether or not someone would go to the holiday dance with you?

If you've been through any of these situations, or similar ones, you've no doubt experienced stress. This short-term kind of stress, though, can be thought of as good stress, because it produces energy that keeps you alert and ready to do what you need to do. In cases like these, stress is useful, and sometimes absolutely necessary. If a car pulls out in front of you and you have to slam on the brakes to avoid hitting it, it's stress that helped you to react quickly and do what was necessary to prevent a potentially serious accident.

Bad stress, on the other hand, occurs when a stressful situation is acute or continues over time. This could happen if your parents aren't getting along and you're always on alert, waiting for them to get into another fight. It could be that you've moved to a new school and have become a target for teasing and bullying from kids in your classes. These sorts of situations cause chronic or long-term stress, which can produce very negative results. You'll learn more about the physical and emotional effects of stress in later chapters.

HOW STRESS WORKS

Stress, as it refers to your body's response to particular situations, occurs when something happens that demands extra awareness and action. If you're walking with a friend and a large dog runs out at you, teeth bared and snarling, you're almost sure to feel stress in the form of fear.

At that point, a small part of your brain called the *hypothalamus* sends an alarm, and your body automatically goes into "fight-or-flight" mode, preparing you to protect yourself from the dog by either standing your ground and dealing with it or running as fast as you can away from it. A function of evolution, the fight-or-flight response has helped animals and humans for millions of years to deal with foes by fighting them or by fleeing as quickly as possible to avoid a potentially harmful situation. It causes all sorts of interesting things to happen to your body, which you'll learn more about in chapter 4.

The fight-or-flight response has proven to be incredibly useful through time, and still is in the event that you are chased by a dog or have to swerve to avoid a car accident. The problem, however, is that our bodies become conditioned to shift into this mode even in response to situations that don't require fighting or fleeing, or for which doing either would be highly inappropriate.

Let's say that your teacher approaches you as you're getting ready to leave class and asks you to stay afterward to talk to her. You can only imagine that it's about the test you took earlier that week, and you're terrified that you did poorly on it and it will affect your final grade and probably keep you out of college and your life will be ruined. By this time, your heart is racing, your hands are clammy, you're breathing like you've just run a mile, and you're experiencing all of the other symptoms of the fight-or-flight response. You'd love nothing more than to turn and run out of the room as fast as you can, but you know that's an inappropriate reaction. In reality, though, your teacher only wants to tell you that, because your test grade was only a B-, you should consider doing some extra-credit work in order to improve your overall grade before the marking period ends. This is hardly a situation requiring the fight-or-flight response, but that's how we have become conditioned to react to stressful situations. If those sorts of situations happen too often, or your body for some reason doesn't release the stress and reset itself back to a relaxed state, problems can occur.

STRESS IS NOT A NEW THING

Stress is getting a lot of attention these days as it becomes more commonly experienced at all age levels and more prevalent across society. Neither stress, nor the study of it, however, is new.

The fight-or-flight response outlined above was first described in the late 1920s by Dr. Walter Bradford Cannon, who was chairman of the department of physiology at Harvard Medical School, from which he had graduated, and president of the American Physiological Association. The phrase "fight or flight" was easy to remember, and helped people to understand the physical reaction to stress.

Since Cannon's time, other researchers have refined the fight-or-flight theory by reversing the order of the two reactions and adding a "freeze" stage in front of both. "Freeze, flight, or fight" better describes the biological reaction to stress in both animals and people, according to a group of researchers whose 2004 study results were published in a publication of the Academy of Psychosomatic Medicine.

At about the same time Cannon was working to describe the physical reaction to stress, an Austrian doctor and professor named Hans Selye was studying how stress affected people who were sick or had suffered an injury. Selye discovered that people suffering from diverse illnesses and injuries showed many of the same symptoms, and he concluded this was their bodies' responses to being ill or injured. This response, he concluded, was separate to the actual disease or injury, and was actually a disorder of its own. He called it general adaptation syndrome, and continued to study the causes and results of stress until he died in 1982.

These early researchers set the tone for the volumes of research that have followed, with both privately and publicly funded studies providing increasing amounts of information on how humans are affected by stress, the causes of stress, and how we can work to better deal with it. Researchers with organizations such as the National Institutes of Health, the American Psychological Association, the American Medical Association, the Centers for Disease Control and Prevention, the Mayo Foundation for Medical Education and Research, and many colleges, universities, and other institutions have contributed to ongoing stress research.

THE INCREASING OCCURRENCE OF STRESS AMONG TEENS

Research regarding the causes and effects of stress is increasingly important as health-care professionals become concerned about the high levels of stress among teenagers and people in general. The American Academy of Pediatrics recently issued a report warning that increasing numbers of teens are suffering from anxiety and depression—both of which are linked to stress—and that stress is also manifesting itself as physical symptoms, including headaches, chest pain, sleep disorders, and belly pain.

Finding Reliable Help Online

If you've ever checked out stress-related Web sites, you know there is no shortage of them. Figuring out which sites are useful and reliable, however, can be a little challenging. As a rule, government sites with addresses ending in .gov are considered to be reliable, as are most university and college sites, which have addresses ending in .edu. Make sure, though, that a university address is that of the institution and not a student site, which also may end in .edu. Other reliable Web sites include those of organizations such as the American Psychological Association, the American Psychiatric Association, or Mental Health America, all of which have web addresses ending in .org. Many of these online resources are listed in an appendix in the back of this book. Don't rely on information from Web sites maintained by people who have no training or credentials in managing stress. That's not to say that some such sites do not contain interesting or informative content, but it's difficult to tell whether it's accurate. Avoid sites that offer stress relieving medicines or herbal remedies.

This is a major concern, because we know that long-term stress has negative effects, including digestive difficulties, anxiety, irritability, insomnia, depression, and other problems.

The good news is that the issue of stress among teenagers is being addressed, and professionals and researchers are learning much more about teen stress and how it can be addressed and managed. The American Academy of Pediatrics, for example, has introduced an interactive Web site where teens can design personalized stress-management plans: http://www.aap.org/stress.

WHY AM I MORE STRESSED OUT THAN MY BROTHER?

Caitlin becomes stressed easily—very easily. Somebody can just look at her the wrong way and she can feel her heart beating faster, her anxiety level increasing, and other stress-related symptoms. She has a hard time dealing with her busy schedule, and almost always feels pressured from having too much to do. If Caitlin has a fight with a friend or gets a grade lower than a B on a test, she becomes so distraught that she has trouble leaving the house. Caitlin's brother, Kevin, on the other hand, doesn't seem to worry about anything. He sails along, seemingly content with his average grades and every other aspect of his life. Rarely does anything shake him up or cause him to react in a manner that indicates he feels stressed.

While scientists don't know why some people are so much more affected by stress than others, they do know that people's brains and their endocrine and other systems vary, indicating that there probably are physical causes at work. Certain personalities seem to be more prone to stress than others, and researchers believe there are genetic components to whether someone is stress prone or stress resistant. It also seems clear that life experiences can affect this: For example, people who grow up in nurturing, protective environments tend to experience less stress later in life than those who don't.

If you're a person who experiences stress more easily than others, don't despair or think that your situation is hopeless. You'll learn lots of techniques and tips in this book that will help you recognize the symptoms of stress and to manage your stress.

HOW DOES STRESS AFFECT MY LIFE?

Stress can affect your life in a number of ways. In the form of good stress, it can serve to motivate you and keep you on top of your game. It can encourage you to study hard for that math test, or find time for an extra workout before the cross-country meet.

Too much bad stress, though, especially when it becomes chronic, can result in stress overload, which can affect your ability to be productive and function well. Too much stress over time can make you feel overwhelmed, tired, and irritable, and can lead to some of physical problems mentioned earlier, like digestive issues or headaches. Being frequently or constantly stressed can make it hard to concentrate on everyday tasks such as schoolwork, and can interfere with the relationships you have with others.

You'll learn a lot in this book about the underlying causes of stress, how stress affects people differently, why teens are more prone to stress than almost any other age group, and how to deal with the stress that you can't avoid. It's important to remember that, even if you're feeling overwhelmed by stress, that in most cases there are steps you can take to manage your stress so that it doesn't control your life.

WHAT YOU NEED TO KNOW

- ➤ *Stress* can refer both to the stimulus that causes you to react, and to your reaction to that stimulus.
- ➤ Stress is a normal reaction that nearly everyone experiences when situations occur that are upsetting or that cause us to change course.
- ➤ Good stress is short-term stress that produces energy that keeps you alert and ready to do what you need to do, while bad stress is stress that occurs over time, draining your energy and causing other problems.
- ➤ A stressful situation causes a physical reaction that prepares the body to fight or flee, even when neither of those behaviors is necessary or appropriate.
- ➤ Stress is on the rise among teenagers, causing concern among health-care providers.
- ➤ People react differently to stress, with some able to handle stressful situations more easily than others.
- ➤ It's thought that a variety of factors—genetic, psychological, and environmental—contribute to how an individual reacts to stress.
- ➤ Stress can have both positive and negative effects in your life, so it's important to understand how to keep it under control, and to use it to your advantage when possible.

2

What Causes Stress?

Stress happens to most people on a fairly regular basis, and it comes in many forms. Schoolwork and academic pressures, parents, friends, siblings, peer pressure, dating situations, too many extracurricular activities, societal expectations, financial concerns, job pressures, and dozens of other situations all can be sources of stress.

While common sources of stress have been identified and are pretty much understood, what's harder to explain is why some people seem to be more susceptible to stress than others, and why some situations are big stressors for some people but cause others only very mild stress, or no stress at all. Consider Jodi, for instance, who is fanatical about getting to school on time. It's only a 10-minute walk from her house, but she often gets a ride with a friend because it's quicker that way. If her friend doesn't show up on time, Jodi absolutely panics, grabs her backpack and keys, and takes off running, terrified that the bell will ring before she arrives and she'll be late getting to her homeroom. The thought of being late to school is a huge stressor for Jodi.

Her neighbor, Danny, however, doesn't seem to care at all about getting to school on time. He strolls out the front door and walks leisurely down the street, often finishing his breakfast or drinking a cup of coffee as he goes. If the bell rings before he gets to school it's no big deal, he'll simply get there when he gets there. Even the detentions that have resulted from his tardiness don't seem to cause him much stress. For Danny, the possibility of being late to school is only a little stressor, if it's a stressor at all.

So why is being late for school such a huge deal for Jodi, and not much of a deal at all for Danny? There are a variety of reasons why people react differently to stress and stressors. Some people are simply more hearty and resilient as far as stress is concerned, while others are more sensitive and thin-skinned. It's just one of the ways in which people vary, caused by differences in the brain and endocrine system, which is a set of glands that produce hormones. The hormones go into the bloodstream and are transported to organs and tissues throughout the body, controlling functions including growth, metabolism, and sexual development and function.

If the brain interprets a situation to be a threat, it sends a signal to the endocrine system and the endocrine system prepares the body for its fight-or-flight response. If the brain interprets a situation to be safe, it doesn't alert the endocrine system. Genetics and experiences early in life determine how your brain will interpret different experiences, and you may perceive something to be a threat that someone else perceives to be perfectly safe.

If you were scratched in the face by a cat when you were a small child, for instance, you may have a fear of cats because your brain perceives them to be a threat. Even though you know that cats are not dangerous, the fear you have of them may continue.

A person whose brain is conditioned to perceive many situations as threatening will be more vulnerable to stressors than a person whose brain tends to assess situations as harmless. This means that a person who is abused while growing up probably tends to look at the world as a more dangerous place than someone who has never experienced any type of abuse, and, as a result, experiences more stress.

Military personnel and their families often have trouble when a soldier returns home from active duty in a combat zone because the soldier continues to experience some of the stress that was a constant part of his or her life during the tour. While the family might expect their loved one to give them all a hug, breathe a big sigh of relief to be home, and settle back into the life he had before serving, often that doesn't happen.

The soldier may continue experiencing stress reactions that affect his ability to trust others or to re-establish emotional ties and make him feel irritable, have trouble communicating, have little interest in social or family activities, or remain convinced that something awful is about to happen. That's because his brain has been conditioned over time to perceive nearly every situation as dangerous, and he is ultrasensitive to stressors, even when they are merely perceived, not actual.

People who have been in an accident, a victim of crime or violence, have witnessed a traumatic event, or have been subjected to another

The Amazing Endocrine System

The endocrine system is intricate and amazing in that it affects almost every function, cell, and organ of the body, including the manner in which you react to and deal with stress. You can find out a lot more about the endocrine system and how it works at this Web site from the Nemours Foundation: http://kidshealth.org/teen/your_body/body_basics/endocrine.html

type of bad experience also may continue to experience stress after the experience has ended. In these sorts of cases, it's very important for family members to learn about what's going on with their loved one and to be patient and supportive while urging the loved one to get professional psychological help.

As you read earlier, there also are other reasons why some people seem better equipped to deal with stress, including genetic and environmental factors. While some people are less bothered and affected by stressful situations than others, everyone encounters stress at some point. In this chapter, we'll look at three different types of stress: biological, sociological, and psychological. We'll also look at the sorts of situations—or stressors—that result in those types of stress.

BIOLOGICAL CAUSES OF STRESS

Karen's parents were not overly surprised when she began complaining of headaches when she was still in elementary school. Many of her mother's family also suffered from headaches and were prone to depression. At first, Karen's headaches occurred only now and then, but they became progressively worse through middle school. By the time she was 16 and in high school, she was suffering from frequent migraines that left her virtually incapable of functioning. The better part of each day was spent in bed, her schoolwork suffered badly, and her social life was practically nonexistent.

Although none of the doctors the family consulted could find a medical explanation for Karen's terrible headaches, they caused a lot of physical pain. The doctors had tried different medicines and combinations of medicines for years, but her pain remained. Unable to figure out a reason for the headaches, her doctors simply recommended that Karen not try to force herself to keep up any kind of a normal schedule while she was experiencing pain. As the headaches occurred with greater frequency, Karen spent more and more time in pain, isolated, frustrated, and depressed.

While some people assumed that Karen's headaches had been brought on by stress, that was not the case. In Karen's situation, the headaches were a huge *source* of stress that forced her to alter her activities and the way she lived. Her condition not only caused Karen stress, it was a stressor for other family members, as well.

We tend to take our bodies and health for granted, until something goes wrong. The human body is an incredible machine that operates with amazing accuracy and efficiency, until that function is interrupted by illness or injury. Changes to our bodies resulting from disease or injury can be significant sources of stress. Sickness, ranging in severity from a sore throat to cancer, can generate feelings of fear, anxiety, helplessness, and even hopelessness, all of which increase stress levels. In fact, psychiatrists have cited personal illness as one of the top sources of stress, as it was for Karen and her family.

Jason was diagnosed at age four with cancer in his bladder, prostate, and lungs. He endured surgery and chemotherapy; by the time he was a teenager he was, fortunately, cancer-free. While Jason understands he's extremely fortunate that his cancer was treatable, he suffers a lot of stress from its consequences, as do other members of his family.

He must be tested every six months to make sure the cancer hasn't returned, and he, his parents, brothers, sisters, and friends live with persistent fear that it will. They all try to appear to be upbeat and optimistic at all times, especially as the date for Jason's test gets closer. You can almost tell how close the testing day is by the degree to which family members are forcing themselves to be positive about everything. Additionally, the cancer and treatment caused some physical problems that Jason must deal with, creating a biological condition that results in significant stress. As you might imagine, his family shares his stress.

This recognition of the relationship between physical illness and stress was identified in 1967 by psychiatrists Thomas Holmes and Richard Rahe, who compiled something called the Holmes and Rahe stress scale. The scale is used as a means of predicting whether people who are exposed to traumatic events have a greater possibility of getting sick, and lists personal illness as one of the top sources of stress.

It's problematic that increased stress levels caused by illness or injury can result in even less satisfactory physical health, making an illness even worse or hampering recovery. So you see, there's a two-

Stressors Likely to Lead to Illness

The Holmes and Rahe stress scale identifies the following stressors as the greatest contributors to illness: Death of a spouse or child, divorce, marital separation, serving time in jail, death of a family member, personal illness, marriage, pregnancy, child leaving home, change of school, and carrying a mortgage. Other, less traumatic stressors on the scale include change in social status, change in sleeping habits, and Christmas.

way connection between illness and injury and stress. Illness and injury are sources of stress, or stressors. There is, however, increasing evidence that stress can cause a variety of illnesses, or at least make people more prone to getting certain illnesses. You'll read more about the physical effects of stress in chapter 4 and the long-term physical effects of stress in chapter 6.

ENVIRONMENTAL OR SOCIOLOGICAL CAUSES OF STRESS

When we talk about environmental or sociological causes of stress, we're referring to the stressors that exist within our own worlds. Environmental stress, in this case, doesn't have anything to do with global warming, melting ice caps, rising water levels, or dead zones in the ocean, although you may be concerned about those things to a degree that causes you to feel stressed. For the purposes of this chapter, sociological, or social stressors are situations that occur within our environments, such as difficult term papers, schedules that are too busy, unhappy home situations, problems with friends, romantic problems, economic difficulties, being the target of bullying, learning to drive, having a brother or sister who is very sick, and so on. They are external sources of stress, meaning that they come from sources outside of ourselves.

An extensive survey conducted in 2007 by the Associated Press and MTV revealed that, among 13- to 17-year-olds, school is the most common source of stress. Among 18- to 24-year-olds, most stress is caused by job and financial concerns. Teens also reported feeling stressed about safety in their schools and neighborhoods, and the possibility of terror attacks. Overall, girls experienced more stress associated with safety, and reported feeling less safe in their schools and neighborhoods than boys did. They also worried more about terrorism than boys did. Almost half of all girls polled reported feeling stressed frequently, compared to about one third of all boys. And 85 percent of boys and girls reported feeling stressed at least some of the time.

Teens from urban areas were found to experience more stress than those who live in rural settings. Interestingly, those who lived in middle-income families (families earning between $50,000 and $75,000 a year) reported experiencing more stress than those from either low- or high-income families.

As with biological stressors, social and environmental stressors can range from mild, such as missing the school bus, to terribly serious, such as being the victim of a robbery or rape. While missing the bus might cause you to temporarily become quite anxious, that's a short-term situation that normally is over quickly and pretty much forgotten. Once you figure out how to get to school, you settle down and your system gets back to normal. In extreme cases, however, an incident of great stress will have lasting results, such as post-traumatic stress disorder (PTSD).

Most Americans first heard about PTSD during and after the Vietnam War, when veterans were found to be experiencing the disorder. PTSD, however, does not only result from events that occur during war. It can be triggered by any traumatic event, such as being abused, a car accident, seeing a loved one get seriously injured or killed, a natural disaster, or being abducted.

You'll learn more about PTSD in chapter 5, but, if you feel you may be experiencing this disorder, it's really important to talk to someone who can lead you to help with it.

PSYCHOLOGICAL CAUSES OF STRESS

While social or environmental causes of stress occur externally, or outside of ourselves, psychological stress comes from within, usually caused by expectations we set for ourselves, or the expectations from others that we internalize and make our own.

You've probably been told since the time you were very small that you are expected to behave in a certain manner, to look a certain way, and to achieve certain things. Communication of these expectations isn't always spelled out, but because the messages are drilled into you over and over again, you get the idea.

These messages come from a variety of sources. Your parents and other family members communicate early on how you are to behave. They establish expectations for almost every area of your life, from what kinds of grades you'll earn and what you'll wear, to who your friends will be and who you will date. They might even establish expectations for if and where you'll go to college, what sort of work you'll aspire to do when you graduate from high school or college, and where you'll live as an adult.

If those early expectations are realistic and manageable, they can provide a valuable framework for how you think and behave. You know, for instance, that you're expected to get yourself to school on time, perform to the best of your ability while you're there, and not get into trouble.

If the expectations are unrealistic, however, such as you need to get straight A's, complete all the advanced placement courses you can get, and graduate from high school with a 4.5 cumulative grade average and a semester's worth of college credits—all as you've been establishing a reputation as a premier musician and the best athlete in the county— it's very likely that you'll end up believing that you're a failure because you're not able to achieve the expectations put upon you. A child can quickly get the message that she's a failure, which can negatively affect her self-esteem and possibly cause big problems down the road.

How we are raised greatly affects our perceptions of ourselves. If the people who are important to you have praised you and affirmed your worth, you are likely to feel good about yourself. If, on the other hand, you've been told since you were a baby that you'll never amount to anything, or you're stupid, or incompetent, or lazy, or worthless, you're likely to internalize those messages and believe that's what you are.

Nearly everyone feels from time to time that they're not good enough, or they don't measure up to expectations. This is usually in response to a particular situation, such as being cut from the basketball team, failing a test, or not getting a part in the class play, and it's a temporary situation. Teens who have grown up hearing over and over that they're useless or no good, however, are likely to have trouble changing those perceptions about themselves.

Children who are mistreated, whether physically, emotionally, or sexually, often grow up with a lot of distrust and fear, which can affect their relationships with others and cause a lot of stress. Expectations and beliefs developed early in life have a lot of impact on how someone deals with life.

Your peers also have expectations for how you'll look and behave, and often their expectations clash with those of your parents. This can cause you to feel confused, upset, and angry at either your parents, your peers, or all of them. At the same time, advertisers are working hard to convince you that they know best what you need in order to look good, feel good, and be happy and successful. Your teachers make it clear that they expect you to behave in a certain manner, and they pressure you to keep up with schoolwork and achieve good grades. You might feel pressured by your place of worship to believe and behave in a certain manner. Even clubs and extracurricular activities demand certain traits and behaviors from you.

Although it's completely impossible to live up to every expectation and demand placed upon you, many teens feel pressured to try to do so. They work hard to please their friends, parents, teachers, coaches and advisors, spiritual leaders, and even those advertisers who have convinced them they're looking out for their best interests.

They worry about whether they're good looking enough, popular enough, cool enough, or smart enough. They worry about whether they'll be able to find a job or to get into college, and whether they'll be able to get scholarships to help pay for it. They worry about having too much to do, that they'll disappoint their parents, that their friends won't like them anymore, that they'll never have a good romantic relationship, and on and on and on. Most psychological stressors for teens are the result of expectations they place upon themselves or are placed upon them by others. Other psychological stressors include fears about safety of self and loved ones, including the threat of terrorist attacks.

Your general attitude and outlook on life affects how you react to situations and your vulnerability to stressors. Someone who is optimistic, has healthy self-esteem and is able to deal well with others probably is less vulnerable to stressors than someone who has a general mistrust of the world and others and believes he is not as good as others. People who tend to worry a lot, particularly about situations over which they have little or no control, tend to stress more than those who don't worry as much, or who plan how they'd deal with a bad situation in the event that it would occur.

RECOGNIZING STRESS AND MEETING IT HEAD ON

Nobody ever said (or ever said correctly) that being a teenager is easy. Teens face pressures from parents, peers, teachers, and others on a daily basis. What you believe, how you act, and what you do are frequently challenged. And, at this stage of your life, you're encountering new situations every day, many of which you're not sure how to handle. You might feel like you're not living up to the expectations that others place on you, or that you place on yourself. All of these pressures can result in a high level of stress.

It's important to recognize those things that cause you stress, and to deal with them as they occur instead of pushing them aside and hoping they'll go away. If you're having trouble with a particular class, for instance, and there's a big test coming up that you're really worried about, there are several options for what you can do. You could try to block the test completely from your mind and pretend that it isn't going to happen. Or you can spend every single minute between now and the test studying for it, even though you don't really understand the content on which you'll be tested. A third option would be to go to your teacher, explain that you're having trouble understanding the material that will be on the test and you're concerned that you won't do well, and ask for some extra help.

In most cases, being proactive and addressing a stressful situation is healthier than ignoring it. Unless it's a situation over which you have no control, such as whether your favorite pro team will win its game on Sunday, taking positive action to resolve a problem is usually better than doing nothing.

If you've had a fight with your best friend, for instance, you can sit around and think about how upset you are and how your friend treated you badly. You can stress over whether or not you'll still room together on the ski trip this weekend, or if you'll have to try to find someone else at the last minute. You can even convince yourself that your friend hates, you, that she'll always hate you, and that you'll never have a best friend—or probably any friend—again. Or, you can text your best friend and ask her to call you or get online or meet you someplace so you can talk about what happened. That might be hard to do, because it challenges your sense of pride and can seem embarrassing. But if you don't take the first step, you risk feeling worried and anxious until you and your friend eventually set things right.

An important idea to keep in mind is that sometimes a situation is out of your control, and no matter how stressed you get over it or how much you worry about it, it won't change.

These situations can be a lot more serious than whether or not the Packers will beat the Vikings Sunday afternoon. You can stay up at night worrying that a tornado will hit your area, but all your worrying won't prevent that from happening—it's completely out of your control.

You can, however, control what your and your family's response would be if a tornado were to occur where you live. You can read about tornado response, talk to other family members, and come up with a plan in the event that a tornado is predicted for your area.

A lot of people these days are worrying about the current outbreak of H1N1, also known as the swine flu, which has been declared a flu pandemic. Instead of just worrying, however, you can get on a Web site such as that of the Centers for Disease Control and Prevention, which contains a wealth of information about the flu, how to avoid catching it, what to do if you think you have it, and more.

These are examples of taking action in anticipation of stressful situations, and should help to put your mind at ease and relieve your stress.

WHAT YOU NEED TO KNOW

- ➤ What causes stress for one person may not cause stress for another, for a variety of reasons.
- ➤ There are three main categories of stress: biological, sociological (or environmental), and psychological.
- ➤ Personal illness or injury is a biological stressor, and one of the greatest causes of stress among all types of stressors.
- ➤ Sociological stress, also called environmental stress, comes from sources outside of yourself, such as having too much homework or a fire in your home.
- ➤ Psychological stress is stress that comes from within, usually caused by expectations we set for ourselves, or the expectations from others that we internalize.
- ➤ An incident of great stress can have lasting results, such as resulting in post-traumatic stress disorder (PTSD), which requires professional treatment.
- ➤ It's important to be able to recognize your sources of stress and to deal with them in a positive and mature manner.

Why Teens Are at Risk for Stress-Related Problems

Evelyn is 17 years old and has two part-time jobs and is responsible for helping to care for her younger sister and brothers. School is challenging because she is bussed every day between her home school and the area career technology center, where she's studying cosmetology. If the bus isn't on time she's sometimes late to class, or she misses her ride home after school.

Evelyn is glad to have some income, but her restaurant job means she has to come right home from school, do all her homework and keep an eye on her siblings, and be at work by 6 P.M. If it's busy, she might not get home until past midnight, which, of course, means she's exhausted the next morning.

There's not much time to rest on weekends either, because she works both days in a hair salon to earn some extra money and get some experience that she hopes will help her career.

Evelyn tried to talk to her mom about how stressed out she feels, but since her dad left them her mom isn't very interested in Evelyn's problems. She just tells Evelyn they all need to work hard and Evelyn has nothing to complain about—she should be glad she has a chance to earn some money.

Some days Evelyn feels so tired she can hardly drag herself to class. Other times she'll start crying without even knowing why, or she'll be really nasty to her little sister and brothers—something that didn't used to happen. Her friends have told her she's no fun to be around anymore, which is just as well, since she's too busy to do anything.

Evelyn, of course, is a teenager suffering from an incredible stress load, and she's not alone. Teens are busier than ever, trying desperately to juggle school, work, sports, extracurricular activities, friends, and family relationships and responsibilities. For many, stress is just a normal part of life.

Teens are very much at risk for high levels of stress and stress-related problems. In fact, some doctors feel that teens actually may experience more stress than adults. While all age groups are exposed to stressful situations, there are some special circumstances that make teens more susceptible to stress and the problems that accompany it. In this chapter, we'll look at some of the reasons why many teens are more prone to stress than other age groups, and why it's important for you to be aware of them.

LACK OF CONTROL OVER YOUR ENVIRONMENT

Perhaps one of the most difficult aspects of being a teenager is that incredibly frustrating lack of control over your environment and, consequently, your life. Consider the situations described below. You may find that one (or more) sounds familiar.

Kristin hates her school because different groups of kids don't get along, and there are fights in the cafeteria about twice a week. She's almost afraid to walk from class to class, and more than once has been jostled around in the hallway. She feels like she doesn't fit in with any one group, and she's pretty much on her own. She'd love to find another school, but what is she going to do? Her mom's not about to pick up and move just because she's uncomfortable in school, so she's stuck.

Abe has been miserable since the first day of eighth grade, when a group of kids saw him sitting by himself in the cafeteria and started making fun of him for having no friends. They've kept it up for weeks, and it doesn't stop with teasing. They kick him and try to trip him, call him all kinds of names, and steal stuff from his tray. Lately they've been posting lies about Abe on Facebook, trying to get him into trouble by saying he's been threatening kids at school. Abe has no idea how to handle this situation because he's afraid if he tells anyone what's going on, it will get even worse. He's started making up excuses to miss school, and his grades are starting to show it.

Kevin knows that he is absolutely, positively capable of driving himself and his girlfriend to the Coldplay concert next month, and his girlfriend's parents even said they'd buy him a ticket as his birthday gift. His parents, though, don't want Kevin driving on the expressway at night, and the concert will last too late to get a train back. His friend Jack is going to the concert and driving himself, but his parents said he couldn't take extra passengers in his car, so it looks like the concert isn't going to happen. To make everything even worse, his girlfriend is upset with him because he can't drive, and said she's thinking about going with Evan, who she dated before she and Kevin started going together.

In each of these scenarios, the teen described feels a lack of control over his or her environment, which makes it difficult or impossible to change an undesirable situation. As their situations go on and other situations occur, their stress levels get higher and higher. All of these teens feel like they're boxed in, without the ability to break free and take control of their lives.

Developmentally, the job of teenagers is to break away from their parents in order to achieve independence and be able to live on their

The Generation Gap

You've probably heard of something called the "generation gap," which simply refers to the differences between one age group and another that often result in a lack of understanding between generations. Teenagers can't fully understand the plight of adults, because they haven't yet experienced the adult world. It might be difficult for a teenager to understand why an adult gets so upset about a little scratch or dent on a new car—*I mean, it's got to happen sometime, right?* Adults, for their part, tend to forget, or minimize, or set aside their experiences of youth, making it difficult for them to be understanding of the trials of young people. They forget that just because something that happened to them as a teen doesn't seem important any more, doesn't mean that it wasn't very important to them as it was occurring. When this happens, each generation can end up minimizing the other's stress-causing problems, causing additional stress.

own. As a result, teens struggle with their relationships with parents as they work to become more independent and self-reliant.

The problem is that most teens lack financial and other resources to be able to be independent from their parents, so they're "stuck" between a forced dependence and their desire for independence. Teenagers tend to push the envelope as they fight for increased freedom and privileges, while many parents are inclined to hold their children back in order to protect them. This very common situation can be a great source of stress for both teens and their parents.

The incredibly rapid technological growth we've experienced over the past decades may be the cause of additional stress between many teens and parents. You've probably realized that the way you and your friends communicate is different from the way your parents communicate with each other and with their friends and associates. Many teens prefer to interact with one another by texting or "talking" on My Space or Facebook rather than actually speaking to one another. It's likely that your parents, on the other hand, will pick up the phone and call someone. This means that teens connect with others differently than their parents do. A parent may have trouble understanding how her daughter is a "friend" to someone she's never met, or how her son is "going with" a girl he rarely sees. Your mom might get upset when the two of you go for lunch one day and she notices that you're texting with one hand while eating with the other, all the while keeping up your conversation with her as you make plans for what you'll be doing that evening.

Teens' immediate and practically unlimited access to all kinds of information on the Internet also can be unsettling for parents. You might feel like your parents are too clingy, or that they worry too much about what you're doing on the Internet, or that they're creepy because they want to know about your Facebook friends. Your parents, on the other hand, might fear that access to all that information carries the potential for you to believe you are better prepared for certain situations than you actually may be. Being in possession of a precise driving route from the Empire State Building in New York City to the Golden Gate Bridge in San Francisco, for instance, does not necessarily mean you are qualified or prepared to make that trip. It's difficult to realize that information and experience are very different commodities, and it can be frustrating to think you know how to do something when you actually lack the skills and experience to accomplish the task.

FAMILY PRESSURES

Speaking of parents, you probably already know that parents and other family members can cause a significant amount of stress for teenagers. Again, often this is due to the natural struggle that occurs within families as children grow and mature, as well as environmental factors.

Stress also can mount when parents' expectations for a teenager differ from the teen's expectations. If Mom and Dad assume that you'll finish high school and happily enroll in the college from which they both graduated, but you've already decided that you're going to join the Coast Guard or head down to Australia to work for a year or two, there is likely to be a stressful clash of wills.

Different families have different expectations of their teens in terms of what they should do, and what is the "right" way for them to leave home. In some families, teens are expected to get jobs and contribute to the household income, while for others, college is established as a priority. Some teens may be encouraged to get married and have children, or pressured to get out of the house when they turn 18 and are legally considered adults. These sorts of expectations can result in significant stress if they are not shared by all family members.

When parents are experiencing stress of their own, an increasingly common occurrence during these current times of job loss, financial woes, and even home foreclosures, their stress often gets transferred back onto their children. If your mother loses her job, for instance, it's a pretty sure bet that she will experience a good deal of worry and stress. Not only is she likely to be irritable, which can mean your home life isn't as pleasant as you'd like it to be, she may actually share her concerns with you. As a teenager, you're likely to share her stress, because you have some understanding of the potential implications of a job loss. While your eight-year-old sister continues to play with her friends and watch her favorite TV shows, you might be worrying about whether you'll be able to afford to go to college, or wondering if you should ask for extra hours at your part-time job in order to help out at home.

Family situations can result in stress in other ways, as well. It may be that, instead of a mom and a dad, you have a mom and a step-dad and a dad and a stepmom, or some combination of those. It's estimated that one in every three Americans is a member of blended family. If you are, it means that you're likely to have stepbrothers and stepsisters as well as brothers and sisters, which sometimes results in stressful domestic situations. The loss of a family member causes a great deal of stress, as does a divorce, domestic violence, familial abuse, and other situations.

Even a "good" divorce can be disruptive and stressful for a teen. We'll define a "good" divorce as one in which each parent is respectful of the other and willing to work together for the sake of the children.

While this sort of situation is easier to live with than a bitter, angry relationship between parents, any kind of divorce is likely to cause a teen to feel anxious, angry, and upset.

You might be unsure how the divorce will affect you. Will your dad still pick you up after baseball practice? Where will you sleep when you visit your mom on weekends? What if one of them remarries? Even teens who maintain good relationships with both parents are affected by divorce in ways that can be very stressful.

While many teens live with only one parent due to divorce, others experience the loss of a parent through death, which is extremely stressful. If the death is sudden, you may experience not only sadness, but intense anger. You might feel at some level that you are to blame for the death, or agonize over the fact that you weren't able to say good-bye or tell your parent how you felt about him or her. If the death follows an illness, you're likely to second-guess whether you did everything you should have while your parent was sick, or, if the illness created a particularly difficult situation for you and the rest of your family, you might even feel a little relieved that it has come to an end, and then feel guilty for those thoughts. If the death is a result of suicide, the loss can be particularly devastating, resulting in intense feelings of loss and other, complicated emotions. Often, these feelings are too much for teens to deal with on their own, and counseling is necessary in order for them to recover in a healthy manner.

And, tragically, there are many homes in which teens are victims of abuse or neglect. The abuse may be physical, sexual, emotional or psychological, but all are extremely harmful and can affect not only a teen's current relationship with family members, but future relationships, as well. Children and teens who are abused tend to develop distorted ideas about their value or worth as a person. It's hard to believe otherwise if a parent or other adult repeatedly tells you you're worthless or no good, and these situations create tremendous stress for victims. If you are in a situation where you, or someone else in your home is being abused, it's extremely important that you seek help from a responsible adult, such as a teacher, school nurse, or guidance counselor.

SOCIETAL EXPECTATIONS

Jennifer experienced a major growth spurt when she was in fifth grade, affecting not only how she felt about herself then, but how she still feels about herself now in 11th grade. All of a sudden, she was taller and bigger than everyone else in her class—both boys and girls. She began developing earlier than almost all the other girls, which resulted in a lot of teasing and stares. Her mother explained that girls usually begin to mature physically before boys, and that this growth was normal and other kids would soon catch up, but Jennifer couldn't get over the feeling that she was awkward and freakish.

Sure enough, the other kids caught up and by the time they got to high school Jennifer was again only of average size compared to her peers. Despite that, however, she continues to feel "different" and uncomfortable. She still thinks of herself as being big and misshapen, even though that's not the case at all. Jennifer learned the hard way how difficult it is to be different in our society, which works hard to define how we should look and act.

We're bombarded with advertising that tells us how we can look better, feel better, live better, and be better. After a while, those messages can lead you to believe that you are deficient in some way—just not quite good enough. What you need to understand is that feeling insecure and self-conscious at times is perfectly normal, and not confined to teens. Adults, too, sometimes experience these feelings. We all feel that a lot is expected of us, and we sometimes don't measure up. Those feelings can be extremely stressful.

Perhaps you feel like you're not pretty or handsome enough, or you don't have enough money to buy all the cool stuff you'd like to have. You might wish, like Jennifer did, that your body was different in some way, or feel uncomfortable about physical changes that you're experiencing. You might wish you had better clothes, or your hair was smooth and straight instead of curly, or blonde instead of brown. Maybe you wish that you lived in a more prestigious neighborhood, or that you had cooler friends. You may feel like you're not really good at anything, or that you're not appreciated, or that you can't live up to the expectations placed on you. All of these issues are related to self-esteem, and they are not uncommon.

Self-esteem is the quality of liking yourself. If you have good self-esteem, you feel comfortable with who you are. If your self-esteem is not good, you may doubt your worth, or perceive that you are unliked or unloved.

Nearly everyone would change something about themselves, given the opportunity. If you asked supermodel Gisele Bündchen if she was absolutely satisfied with herself, chances are she'd think of something she would change if she were able to. You might still wish you were three inches taller or that your hips weren't as wide, or that you were more popular in school. Good self-esteem, however, helps you to understand that you have many good qualities that are far more important than your height or body shape or popularity level.

Being comfortable with yourself most of the time can decrease the amount of stress you feel, because you learn to accept yourself and your circumstances, and you stop wishing that you were different.

The truth is that you're fine, just the way you are. As much as advertisers don't want you to believe it, you don't need to wear a size 2, own a Kate Spade pocketbook, or look like one of the Jonas brothers in order to be happy and successful. Learning to recognize these societal expectations of how you should look, feel, and act for what they are, and realizing that you don't need to, and probably can't, live up to them, will help you accept yourself as you are.

Some teens, like Matt, experience a lot of stress related to learning problems. Matt enjoyed school in the early years, especially art and music classes. As the work got more difficult and more reading and writing was required, however, he found it harder and harder to keep up. Eventually, he was identified as having a learning disability and placed in a morning support class.

While the class helped him academically, it was a great source of stress for him because he felt singled out and labeled, and other kids made fun of him. Matt knew that reading and writing were difficult for him, but after he was identified as learning disabled he began to feel that he was stupid and inferior. He began acting out in class and gained a reputation for being a troublemaker. Only after he got to high school and was able to attend the career and technology center did he begin to feel like he belonged and was able to relax.

It's difficult to feel like you're different or don't measure up to societal standards whether those involve appearance, learning aptitude, social standing, or something else. And feeling this way is likely to trigger stressors that can be hard to deal with.

PEER PRESSURES

Peer pressure among teenagers probably has existed for as long as there have been teenagers. Your peers are your friends, your classmates, other members of groups or teams to which you belong, the other kids in your neighborhood, and so forth, and they all influence you in some way. Peer influence and peer pressure can be factors in determining what you wear, with whom you hang out, how you speak, what you eat for lunch, where you shop, and many other aspects of your life.

There's a difference between positive peer influence and peer pressure, which is generally perceived to be negative. Peers influence each other positively in many ways. You might have a friend who encouraged you to try out for the class play, even though you didn't think you'd get a part, or who listened as you talked about a problem you were having, or who helped you to study for your algebra test. You and some of your peers might help out at a food bank or homeless shelter, or train together in order to improve your cross-country times.

Positive peer influence is healthy and useful as you work toward becoming independent of your parents. Your peers help you to navigate your world and shape your values. They provide feedback, encouragement, and advice, along with opportunities for social occasions. Many teens are more comfortable with peers than with their families, or at least perceive their peers to be nearly as important to them as family.

Peer influence can become a problem and a cause of significant stress, however, when it turns into peer pressure. Peer pressure occurs when you feel that you should or even have to do something that you don't want to because a friend or another peer is pressuring you to. It can be as benign as feeling pressured to buy a certain brand of jeans, or as dangerous as using drugs or engaging in unprotected sex. Some common forms of peer pressure include:

▸ Pressure to be in a relationship, even if it's not a good one
▸ Pressure to act and look older than you are, even when you don't want to
▸ Pressure to be sexually active, even if don't want to be and your parents don't want you to be
▸ Pressure to use drugs, even though you know it's dangerous and illegal
▸ Pressure to spend more money than you know you should
▸ Pressure to be constantly available to friends through texting and emails, which can interfere with homework, time with family, and other activities

Almost everyone is affected by peer pressure to some degree, although some people are able to handle it better than others. A teen who is confident and has good self-esteem will have an easier time telling a friend that he can't go out to dinner because he doesn't have any money, for example, or that she isn't going to Aaron's party because she knows his parents are away and there's going to be alcohol and drugs present, than one who is insecure and wants very badly to be accepted, regardless of the cost.

Dealing with peer pressure is stressful on several levels. It's difficult to stand up to a friend and refuse to do something. You risk disappointing or angering the friend, and perhaps even losing the friendship, and that can be very upsetting.

On the other hand, engaging in behavior that you know is not safe or advisable might seem exciting at the time, but is likely to cause a good deal of stress later on. And the more risky or "wrong" the behavior is, the greater the degree of stress experienced is likely to be. If, for instance, you agree to use drugs because you think they'll provide quick gratification and make you feel more cool and accepted, you're not only opening the door for serious problems down the road, but you'll probably feel a great deal of stress about getting caught or becoming addicted.

Learn to recognize peer pressure and how it makes you feel. If you're in a situation that doesn't feel right to you, it probably isn't right. You can save some stress by having a plan in place to deal with peer pressure when it does occur. If someone is pressuring you to do something you know is unwise, unsafe, or just not right, being at least somewhat prepared can be helpful.

Anticipate what kinds of peer pressure might occur and when. If you're going to a party and suspect there will be alcohol or drugs there, you might be setting yourself up for some peer pressure. The same applies to dating someone who you think might pressure you for sex, shopping with someone who might think it would be fun to shoplift, and a variety of other situations.

Rehearse ahead of time how you'll deal with peer pressure. If a friend is insisting that you drink a shot at a party, have an answer prepared. You might simply say "No, I don't want to." If you feel like you need an excuse, tell him that your parents wait up until you get home and would know that you'd been drinking, or that your football coach will find out and you'll be thrown off the team. Make up your mind that you won't cave in, no matter how much pressure your friend gives you or how uncomfortable the situation is. Thinking about it ahead of time will help you to decide how you'll act and what you'll do.

Have a backup plan. Unfortunately, circumstances sometimes get out of control, and you could find yourself in a very uncomfortable or even dangerous situation. Make an arrangement with a parent or other trusted adult for a no-questions-asked, immediate bailout plan. You might agree on a special word or phrase you can use to communicate that you're in trouble and need help. For instance, if you're at a party and there is drug use and drinking and you want to leave but don't have a safe ride, you could call your mom and tell her you have a "really bad headache" and need to come home, knowing she will understand that means you need to get out of there quickly. She might be upset with you for going to the party in the first place, but she'll be glad that you took steps to remove yourself from the situation and keep yourself safe. If a situation is really out of control and you are in immediate danger, call 911.

At one time or another, peer pressure is a problem for nearly every teenager. It takes courage to resist peer pressure, but the more often you stand up for yourself and for what you know is right, the easier it becomes. You also can help others to deal with peer pressure by aligning yourself with someone who is trying to do the right thing by resisting pressure.

NEW SOURCES OF PSYCHOLOGICAL STRESS FOR TEENS

Before September 11, 2001, terrorism in the United States was sort of a far-fetched, alarmist concept. Sure, we'd experienced terrorist acts before—the World Trade Center bombing in 1993 in which six people were killed and 1,000 injured; the bombing of a federal building in Oklahoma City in 1995 that killed 166 people and injured hundreds more; violence at clinics where abortions are provided; and other incidences. And we knew that large-scale terrorist acts have occurred with regularity in some other parts of the world for decades. No one, however, was prepared for the homeland horrors of 9/11, and for many people, those events ignited a new type of psychological stressor that has become widespread: fear of terrorist acts.

At the same time, many areas across the United States, including perhaps where you live, have become increasingly unsafe, and we hear more and more about the need to be vigilant in order to stay safe. You might encounter gangs and gang-related violence or other crime in your neighborhood, or read about it in your local newspaper. You may even be a victim of violence, at home or elsewhere.

You might worry about the effects of environmental issues such as climate change or pollution, or wonder if you'll be able to afford to buy gas when you finally get your own car. Perhaps economic pressures are causing you to fear you won't be able to go to college, or your parents will have to sell their house to pay for tuition. Some teens worry that their families will be broken apart due to immigration enforcement, while others fear harm to a loved one serving in a war zone.

These sorts of stressors don't only affect teenagers, but, coupled with all the other stressors teens experience, they can add up and can result in big problems over time. But they also can be addressed and managed, at least to some degree. One way in which you might help yourself is to get involved with a group or organization in your area that is working to combat some of these problems. All over the country, groups of activists are working to make their neighborhoods, communities, country, and world a better place to live. You might join a neighborhood watch group that works to deter crime, or a peace group that works to promote better understanding among community members, or an environmental group that cleans up the streams that run through your area, or an organization that works to care for women who are victims of abuse. You could volunteer in a soup kitchen or homeless shelter. Getting involved and working for change is a good means of addressing your stress head-on and taking some action.

There are many reasons why teens are at risk for stress and stress-related problems, some of which are more easily addressed than others. While you can't eliminate the situations that cause stress, you can learn to deal with that stress in as healthy a manner as possible.

WHAT YOU NEED TO KNOW

> Teens are at risk for stress and stress-related problems and may actually experience as much, and perhaps even more stress than adults.

> Lack of control over many aspects of their environments is a major reason why teens experience stress.

> Family pressures, including misunderstandings between parents and teens, illness, divorce, and death can cause large amounts of stress.

> Social expectations of how you are expected to look or act also can result in stress.

> Peer pressure can be incredibly stressful, and affects nearly every teen to some extent.

➤ Today's teenagers have grown up with terrorism and other forms of violence, all of which can result in raised stress levels over long periods of time.
➤ Stress and stressful situations cannot be avoided, but can be managed in as healthy a manner as possible.

4 ▌▌▌

How Stress Affects You Physically

Imagine this: You and your friend are walking home from school. As you pass by a house you notice a large dog lying on the step outside of the front door. You've never seen this dog before, and you start feeling just a little bit nervous because it doesn't look like the dog is tied to any thing. All of a sudden, the dog charges off the step and runs at you and your friend, its teeth bared and snarling. You and your friend scream and take off as fast as you can, even after you can see that the dog stopped at the edge of its yard and isn't chasing you. You and your friend are both so scared that you're practically crying, and it's a long time until you can fully relax. You vow that you'll never walk past that house again, and the next day you find a new route home from school.

What happened during that incident was that you and your friend experienced a full dose of physical reaction to stress. Stress, as it refers to your body's response to particular situations, occurs when something happens that causes you to change course or that demands extra awareness. You felt stress in the form of intense fear and you responded with an intense physical reaction.

In this chapter we'll examine that physical reaction to stress, and how stress affects the body. Nearly everyone experiences some stress on a regular basis, and, hopefully, our bodies are able to deal with that stress and then rebound back to normal. When stress becomes chronic and long term, however, it can result in a variety of physical problems.

PHYSICAL REACTION TO STRESS

Consider the charging-dog scenario described above, and try to imagine how you really would feel if you experienced a menacing dog running at you, looking as if it intended to attack. Chances are that you're feeling a little bit nervous just thinking about it! When you encounter a somewhat stressful situation, such as a having to cross a busy street, or shoot a foul shot during a close basketball game, or present a book talk in English class, you're likely to experience a physical reaction. You might feel a bit of perspiration under your arms, or your face gets hot, or your palms are sweaty; you feel a little anxious and nervous in general. These responses give you a little extra energy, help you to feel more alert, and generally keep you on your toes. When everything is working properly, a reverse procedure will occur when the stressful situation ends, and your body will return to a relaxed state.

In a serious situation such as a snarling dog running at you, however, your body goes into "fight-or-flight" mode, which prepares you to try to protect yourself from the dog by either standing your ground and dealing with it, or running as fast as you can to get away from it. Several physical reactions occur when this happens; they are known collectively as the stress response.

When your body responds physically to stress, several actions occur. Your brain sends a quick message down your spinal cord to the adrenal glands, signaling the glands to release a good dose of a hormone called adrenaline. Adrenaline increases blood pressure and blood sugar levels and makes your heart beat faster, all of which are advantageous in the event that you need to fight or flee.

While your adrenal glands are working hard to produce adrenaline, a central area in your brain called the hypothalamus and the pituitary gland also are working to trigger the release of hormones, including an important one called cortisol. Stress isn't the only trigger that causes cortisol to be released into the bloodstream, but cortisol has become known as the stress hormone because it occurs at higher levels during stressful situations. Cortisol helps the body to metabolize glucose, regulate blood pressure, maintain blood sugar levels, boost immune function, and respond to inflammation. It also helps your body to maintain its internal balance (this is called homeostasis), and it regulates fluid and electrolyte levels.

During times of stress, cortisol, like adrenaline, helps your body to get ready to do what it needs to do in order to protect yourself or

The Danger of Constant Stress

People who are constantly exposed to stressful situations develop physical problems because their stress response systems are almost always active, resulting in overexposure to cortisol and other stress hormones. Constant exposure to stress hormones can disrupt the normal systems of the body and lead to a variety of ailments, including heart disease, sleep problems, depression, memory problems, skin conditions, obesity, and digestive problems. Some scientists even feel that too much stress can contribute to cancer.

someone else, by making sure that your blood sugar remains high and your blood pressure is elevated.

When you're faced with a stressful situation, your body responds by preparing your brain and muscles to deal with it. Your body's stress response, as it prepares itself for "fight-or-flight" mode, includes a number of responses:

➤ Your heart pumps at two to three times its normal pace, sending increased amounts of blood into the muscles of your arms and legs.
➤ Your eyes dilate, enabling you to see better.
➤ Your blood pressure increases dramatically because the tiny blood vessels just under your skin shut down. This inhibits bleeding in the event that you are wounded.
➤ Your digestive and reproductive systems shut down so that energy can be diverted to other areas of the body. Excess waste may be expelled so that you can run faster.

All of these changes give you an edge and enable you to be stronger and faster than you would be under normal circumstances. It's thought that this is why people are sometimes able to perform extraordinary feats, such as lifting a car off of a person who is trapped or setting a new world's record in the high jump. These responses to stress and danger have helped humans to survive and prosper.

THE CAVEMAN AND THE WILD BEAST

If the thought of a snarling dog seems frightening, imagine that you're a caveman or cavewoman, minding your own business and picking some berries one day, when a large, angry beast emerges from the bushes, intent on finding itself a meal. There's nobody else around, so you're going to have to handle this situation on your own. Luckily, your body automatically responds in a manner that might allow you to escape the beast and live to tell the tale. Scientists think that the fight-or-flight response is an important factor in the evolution of man, and an important tool in the fight for survival.

Those who escaped the wild beasts would head back to their caves, where they would take a long nap, resting and enabling their bodies to return to a normal, relaxed state. Survivors were able to produce offspring with even more developed fight-or-flight responses, which allowed them to deal even better with dangerous situations and continue the evolutionary process.

WHEN PHYSICAL RESPONSE TO STRESS BECOMES A PROBLEM

A physical response to stress is a necessary and useful feature that has served humans well for thousands of years. But sometimes our stress response can be a bad thing. Early humans were surrounded by danger and stress. In addition to wild beasts, there were periods of famine, threats to offspring, environmental stressors such as heat and drought, and other factors that required humans to constantly be on guard and able to react to danger.

In some parts of the world, humans still face those sorts of conditions because of war, or inequitable food distribution, or tyrannical leaders, or other factors. In our society, however, most of us don't face these sorts of perils on a daily basis. Sure, you experience stress when you ask somebody you like to go to see a movie with you, or when you don't have your homework finished and the teacher calls on you to explain how you solved a problem. And every now and then a snarling dog might run at you, or you're involved in a car accident, or you experience some other serious situation.

The problem is that even though we no longer often need the physical responses that saved us from being mangled or devoured in the past, they keep on kicking in. So when the teacher calls on you and you know you're in trouble, your heart beats faster, your blood pressure increases, blood gets pumped to the muscles in your arms and legs, and all those other responses kick in to prepare you to fight or flee.

Your teacher, however, isn't interested in fighting you, although he or she may want to know why you didn't do your homework. And running out of the room would certainly be overly dramatic and unnecessary. So, you sit there with your face red and your heart pounding, sweating, and your stomach churning, unable to act on your instincts to do something more.

Worse still, if you also didn't do your homework for your next class either, the same thing could repeat itself just a half hour or hour later—meaning that your body would maintain that high level of alertness and readiness to fight or run.

If this happens frequently and over a period of time, it can have a negative effect on your body, both short term and long term. Short-term effects of stress include fatigue, an inability to concentrate, sweating, an increased heart rate, abdominal pain, irregular bathroom habits, and anger.

It's important to understand that people react differently to stress, and experience a variety of physical reactions when confronted with stress. Jamal, for instance, has a problem with heavy perspiring when he becomes stressed and anxious, while Megan's stress presents physically as intestinal problems.

Jamal has always been shy and awkward in social situations. He's fine when it's just him and his family, or when he's just with a couple of close friends, but he's very uncomfortable around people he doesn't know. Because of this, he works hard to avoid calling attention to himself and tries to stay in the background. Sometimes, however, that's impossible, and Jamal finds he must interact with others in social settings. The thought of having to deal with social gatherings is so stressful to him that he becomes quite anxious and worried.

As soon as he begins to feel anxiety associated with social occasions, Jamal starts to perspire. He understands that this is an inherited characteristic, because his father has the same condition, but that doesn't make it easier for him. Once he starts to perspire, he becomes even more anxious and worried because he's afraid that other people will notice the problem. Jamal experiences a vicious cycle of worrying, which leads to sweating, which leads to even more worry. On several occasions Jamal has experienced full-blown panic attacks as a result of this condition.

Like most teens, Megan worries about dating and social situations. This is perfectly understandable because forming and developing personal and romantic relationships is a new set of circumstances for teens, and it can be uncomfortable and stressful. What sets Megan apart is her physical reaction to this stress, which shows up in the form of intestinal problems. When she worries that her boyfriend is going to cheat on her or break up with her she experiences cramps, diarrhea, and problems with gas. By her early teens she had already developed irritable bowel syndrome, which caused even more anxiety and angst.

As soon as she begins experiencing symptoms she retreats to her room, which means she's missed some school and a number of activities that she would have liked to participate in. That makes her even more upset, which only makes the problem worse.

Jamal and Megan experience similar feelings of stress and anxiety, but their physical reactions are different. Someone else might respond physically to stress with a headache, or increased incidence of acne, or trouble sleeping.

While stress is the cause of a variety of short-term problems, it also has long-term effects, which can be extremely serious, ranging from cardiovascular disease to some kinds of cancers. Long-term stress also can lead to anxiety, depression, gastrointestinal disorders, ulcers, colitis, and sleep disorders. High stress levels also are linked to immune system–related problems such as frequent colds and infections, and higher incidences of migraines and asthma. People who are exposed to frequent or constant stress, such as those who are being physically or sexually abused, suffering from a serious illness, living in fear of violence in their homes or neighborhoods, or experiencing poverty are more prone to these long-term physical problems. You'll learn a lot more about the long-term effects of stress in chapter 6.

For now, let's consider some of the short-term physical effects, some of which you may have already experienced, and which could be early symptoms of problems resulting from stress over a long period of time.

Gastrointestinal problems. It's not hard to understand how stress is related to gastrointestinal problems. Did you ever start feeling sick in your stomach when you were nervous or anxious? You might have heard someone say that they had "a knot in their stomach" due to being nervous or under stress. Children sometimes develop stomachaches when anticipating an unpleasant situation. Stress has been linked to gastrointestinal disorders such as irritable bowel syndrome, stomach ulcers, and colitis. Short-term effects include stomach cramps, diarrhea, gas, and irregular bowel movements.

Sleeping problems. It's hard for most people to get to sleep when they're really worried or anxious about something. Furthermore, researchers believe that, in addition to mental activity that makes it difficult to sleep, stress hormones designed to rev up the system in preparation for flight or fight contribute to sleeping problems for people who are experiencing a lot of stress. One problem is that someone who is having trouble sleeping at night is likely to be more stressed during the day, which leads to even more sleeping problems at night.

Skin problems. It's clear that stress contributes to skin problems, including acne, hives, eczema, psoriasis, rosacea, and alopecia (loss of hair). Again, stress hormones are thought to have the ability to increase oil production, possibly trigger the body's autoimmune reaction, and otherwise affect the skin, causing problems that range from occasional flare-ups of problems to chronic situations. You may have noticed that your face is more likely to break out when you're anticipating final exams, or the basketball game against your school's top rival, or a visit to traffic court after you were pulled over for speeding.

Perspiring. Excessive sweating is not an uncommon reaction to stress, and it can lead to even greater anxiety. The condition of excessive sweating is called hyperhidrosis, and it's estimated that 2 to 3 percent of the general population are affected by it. Some people with this condition experience underarm sweating, while others sweat excessively from their hands or feet. While stress can contribute to this condition, there can be other medical reasons for it. Hyperhidrosis can be treated with certain over-the-counter antiperspirants, prescription antiperspirants, or medication. In rare cases, a doctor will recommend endoscopic thoracic sympathectomy, a surgery that removes or blocks the nerves that cause sweating in order to inactivate them. While it is considered an effective treatment for hydrosis, and less-invasive surgical techniques have greatly minimized its risks it is not considered as a first line of defense.

Immunity issues. Did you ever notice that you seem to be more susceptible to getting sick when you're under a lot of stress? That's because you really are. High stress levels are linked with problems with the immune system, which, when functioning properly, enables you to fight off colds and other problems. Researchers think that stress-related hormones interact with substances in the body that trigger the immune system, causing the system to be less effective. This makes it more difficult to fight off conditions like the flu, a cold, or an infection.

Headaches. Stress can contribute to migraine headaches as well as the more common tension headaches you may have experienced. The hormones that prepare a person for flight or fight also can cause changes in blood vessels that result in migraines. Tension headaches occur either occasionally or on a regular basis. Occasional tension headaches are known as episodic headaches and can be caused by one stressful occurrence or by stress that builds up over time. Usually they are of short duration and can be treated with over the counter pain relievers. Continual headaches are called chronic tension headaches and may require treatment in the form of stress-management counseling, biofeedback, or medications.

Sexual dysfunction. When someone is under a lot of stress, the hormones that regulate the reproductive system can be inhibited, leading to sexual dysfunction.

WHAT YOU NEED TO KNOW

- A physical reaction to stress can help you to perform better by providing extra energy and increased awareness and alertness.
- Physical response to stress includes increased heartbeat and blood pressure, dilated pupils, greater blood flow to muscles, enhanced memory, and a temporary shutdown of the digestive and reproductive systems, preparing the person for a fight-or-flight response.
- Hormones, including cortisol, get released into the body during times of stress.
- The body's physical response to stress has evolved over time, and it was extremely useful to humans who were surrounded by constant danger and stresses such as drought or hunger.
- While physical response to stress can be valuable and necessary, it often occurs even when it's not needed.
- Different people respond physically to stress in a variety of ways, such as headaches, stomach problems, or excessive sweating.

➤ There are both short- and long-term physical responses to stress, and short-term responses can be early symptoms of long-term problems.

➤ Long-term or constant physical response to stress can cause problems and illnesses such as cardiovascular disease, gastrointestinal disorders, headaches, sleeping problems, and skin problems, among others.

How Stress Affects You Emotionally

Just as your body responds physically to stress, it also responds emotionally. When confronted with a stressful situation you might feel anxious, or panicky, or filled with dread. You may even feel confused, or like you can't deal with what's going on. Some people withdraw when facing a stressful situation, while others act out.

An emotional response to stress, also called a psychological response, can be immediate and very strong, just as a physical response can be.

Madison was thrilled when she was named head twirler of her high school's band front. She soon found out, however, that performing in that role made her incredibly nervous and stressed out. In addition to physical symptoms like excessive sweating, a pounding heart, and feeling sick to her stomach, she had strong emotional symptoms of anxiety and fear. She reacted both physically and emotionally to the stress that resulted from performing in front of a crowd of people.

And, just as long-term or chronic stress can cause physical problems, emotional problems can result as well, and can continue long after the source of the stress has stopped.

The Centers for Disease Control and Prevention (CDC) lists emotional responses that commonly occur following a traumatic or otherwise extremely stressful event. The responses include anxiety, guilt, grief, denial, severe panic, fear, anger or irritability, loss of emotional control, depression, sense of failure, feeling overwhelmed, and blaming others or oneself.

Let's look at some of these emotional responses to stress and how they can affect not only the person experiencing the stress, but family and friends as well.

FEAR AND ANXIETY

Fear and anxiety are very common and real reactions to stress. The two are closely related and often occur together. Consider the following scenario: Rob and his buddy Zack are driving back from a baseball game in a large city about an hour from their homes. It's dark, and they're not very familiar with the area, so they miss the turn to get back onto the expressway out of the city and end up in a bad part of town. They know that this area is known for gangs and violence, and they are understandably scared. Scared turns into really scared, even terrified, when they stop at a red light and three guys start walking quickly toward their car, one of them carrying what appears to be a crowbar.

At this point, Rob and Zack are experiencing both physical and emotional reactions to their situation. The instinctual fear they feel invokes the fight-or-flight reaction that you read about in chapter 4. And, that reaction is coupled by intense emotional responses of anxiety and trepidation. Both their physical and emotional reactions are perfectly normal and warranted by their circumstances.

Once they escape from immediate danger by pulling away from the light and getting themselves back on track and on the way home, they begin to relax. Their stress lessens and their anxiety subsides.

Rob moves on, and a few days later is joking and laughing about the incident. Zack, however, can't get over the feeling that something bad is going to happen. He's afraid he's going to get lost again, and is reluctant to drive anywhere not completely familiar to him. He sees people who remind him of the men who approached his car and can feel himself getting anxious and afraid. His head pounds, he breaks out in a sweat, waves of fear wash over him, and he feels like he's going to completely lose control. His stress is compounded by the fact that Rob jokes about the incident and tells Zack that he's got to get over it and quit acting like such a wimp.

Zack is no longer experiencing instinctual fear, because there is no real and present danger. He is, however, experiencing a lot of stress in the form of anxiety.

One of the problems with anxiety is that it tends to feed on itself. When Zack is reminded of that night, he experiences great anxiety, to the point of feeling like he's losing control. Knowing that he's likely to experience that feeling the next time he's reminded of the incident makes him even more anxious, because he worries about what he might do or how he will react.

Several months later, Zack finally talks to his mother about what happened and how he's feeling, and his mom, who's noticed that Zack has been upset and anxious, makes an appointment for him to see a counselor. Now Zack has been diagnosed with an anxiety disorder, and possible post-traumatic stress disorder.

POST-TRAUMATIC STRESS DISORDER (PTSD)

Post-traumatic stress disorder (PTSD) is an anxiety disorder that sometimes occurs following a traumatic experience, such as a serious car accident, abuse, natural disaster, war, an abduction, or assault. Although it's not a normal reaction, any teen could experience this condition following a very traumatic event. It's not fully understood why some people experience PTSD while others do not.

It's believed that, while trauma triggers the anxiety disorder, genetics helps to determine why only certain people will experience PTSD. In the situation described above, for instance, Zack and Rob experienced the same trauma, but Ron easily recovered from it while Zack did not.

There are three main symptoms that indicate PTSD:

▸ Flashbacks or nightmares in which you relive the traumatic event
▸ A constant or recurring feeling of emotional numbness
▸ A need to avoid people, places, or events associated with the trauma

While those are considered common symptoms, not everyone who has PTSD will experience them or react to their experience in the same way. Younger children tend to seek comfort from family members, and may regress in development or become afraid of situations that have nothing to do with the traumatic event they've experienced. Teens are more likely to experience these symptoms, and can experience a variety of reactions, including anxiety, depression, anger, feelings of isolation, and self-destructive behaviors. They may have flashbacks and nightmares in which they relive the trauma, and become withdrawn and unable to enjoy every day activities.

Anniversaries of the traumatic event can trigger great anxiety, as can anything that reminds them of the event.

Symptoms of PTSD usually begin to appear within three months of the traumatic experience, and last for at least a month. In rare cases, however, PTSD won't become apparent until years after the experience.

PTSD may improve on its own over time, but many people suffering from it will continue to have problems for a long time. Unfortunately, PTSD can even become a chronic condition. If you've experienced a traumatic event, you can probably expect that things will be difficult for a while. Try not to be overly hard on yourself by thinking that you should be able to shake off your feelings or "snap out" of a mood. Be sure that you take care of yourself by eating regular, healthy meals, getting enough sleep, and staying in touch with family and friends. Chances are, you'll gradually start to feel better and more like your old self.

If you think you may have PTSD, it's important to ask a trusted adult for help. Tell the person how you're feeling, and why you think you might be experiencing PTSD. The disorder is easier to treat if it's recognized early.

PTSD often can be treated effectively with a combination of medications and psychotherapy, particularly cognitive-behavioral therapy, which involves working with both thoughts and behaviors. Therapy typically would begin with having the teen talk about the traumatic event. The therapist may offer some assertiveness training and relaxation techniques to help the teen sort out confusing thoughts about the event and to better manage anxiety. PTSD can be a serious problem, but many teens have been successfully treated for it.

ANGER AND IRRITABILITY

Sarah was shocked when her parents sat her and her brother down one night and told them they were going to get divorced. She knew that things hadn't been great between them for a while, but her dad had been working lots of nights and wasn't around much during the week. When he was home on weekends, she usually was out with her friends, so she hadn't experienced many of their conversations, fights, or long periods of silence.

While Sarah's initial reaction to her parents' announcement was intense sadness, she soon became angry—and she remained angry for months. Whenever she thought about the divorce, she felt furious.

She stopped talking to both of her parents, blaming them for ruining her life. She slammed doors shut as she came in and out of the house, and refused to clean up after herself or follow other house rules. She acted out by spending time with a group of classmates who were into smoking and drinking, staying out late, and not letting her parents know where she was.

Sarah's intense anger eventually lessened, and her mother convinced her to enter counseling, which she did. In time, Sarah understood that her behavior, although understandable, had not been productive, and she started working to make the unfortunate situation of her parents' divorce as tolerable as it could be.

Anger and irritability are common emotional reactions to stress. Some people, like Sarah, act on their anger, while others become withdrawn and quiet. Sometimes a person may not even realize that she's very angry until that anger suddenly and unexpectedly surfaces.

While Sarah acted on her anger, her brother, Stephen, reacted by becoming very quiet and withdrawn. He'd go directly to his room when he came into the house, declining to eat dinner with Sarah and their mom. He stopped participating in activities he used to enjoy, preferring to spend time by himself, playing video games or surfing the Internet. He stopped doing his homework and his grades dropped dramatically. His friends tried to convince him to come out and do something with them, but Stephen made excuses and stayed in his room. In time, Stephen did come out of his room, and he too entered counseling.

Both Stephen and his sister Sarah were angry about the situation, but their responses to their anger were very different. As they became more accustomed to their new situation and used to the idea of the divorce, their anger subsided and they were able to resume their normal behavior.

While Sarah's aggression was a means of expressing her anger, aggression sometimes occurs for other reasons. Scientists think there is a genetic link to aggression. Some researchers have cited social causes, such as watching a lot of violent movies or playing violent video games, but that theory is disputed. Some medications can cause aggressive behavior, as can certain medical conditions.

There also are a variety of explanations for withdrawn behavior, including certain psychiatric conditions, depression, extreme shyness, physical illness, certain medications, behavioral problems, and emotional abuse.

SENSE OF FAILURE

Brittany lives with a father who sets impossibly high standards for his children and is emotionally abusive when they don't live up to those standards. He is a very successful businessperson and highly respected for the community and humanitarian work he does, but he has caused a lot of damage to his kids.

Brittany is smart and works hard in school. Because she is 16, however, she obviously doesn't have the business or life experiences of her father. When Brittany doesn't know how to handle a particular situation or doesn't know the answer to a question, her father becomes enraged, telling her in a variety of ways that she's stupid. She's a failure who doesn't know anything or can't do anything right, he says. Brittany used to try to seek his advice on different matters, but there's no way she'd ask him anything now, because—according to him—she's supposed to already know everything. Brittany deals with her dad by ignoring him as much as possible, but, after hearing it so many times from her father, Brittany has a hard time thinking of herself as anything but a stupid failure. She's convinced that she can't do anything right, that she doesn't know anything, and she won't succeed in life because she doesn't have the necessary skills or abilities. She's become extremely depressed as a result of these feelings, and recently approached her mother, who set up an appointment for Brittany to get some professional help. As with cases of PTSD, cognitive-behavioral therapy is the most effective approach to treating Brittany's sense of failure and depression.

DEPRESSION

Jack, 15, is a perfectionist. He also suffers from depression, brought on by the stress and frustration that results from his feeling that no matter what he does, it, or he, is never good enough. It doesn't matter to him that he made the varsity golf team as a freshman; he believes he should have been the top player instead of number three. It doesn't matter that he's in the top 10 percent of his class academically; he thinks he should be the highest-ranked student. Jack often feels angry at himself, or that he doesn't like himself, because he can't meet the high expectations he's placed on himself.

His parents want Jack to do well, but they're very worried that he's so unhappy, and they notice that he's beginning to spend more time in his room and seems to be experiencing problems sleeping.

Knowing that Jack may have inherited certain genes that make him vulnerable to depression, and that he experiences a tremendous amount of stress because of his perfectionist tendencies, they decide to have Jack undergo a psychiatric evaluation, which confirms the depression.

Stress affects the body's hormone levels, and this, in a susceptible person, can lead to depression. It could be that, like Jack, you're putting too much pressure on yourself, or, like Brittany, someone else is placing unrealistic expectations on you. All types of stress can contribute to the development of depression, including the loss of a loved one; the breakup of a relationship; sexual, physical, or emotional abuse; severe school-related pressure, or other pressures; or a troubled family situation.

While stress certainly plays a role in depression, most experts agree that major depression is caused by a combination of brain chemistry, genetics, and your emotional environment. Other factors that can contribute to depression include illness, diet, medications, and substance abuse.

Depression is common, and can be successfully treated. The first step in getting better is to get help, so if you feel that you may be suffering from depression, don't hesitate to ask for help. As with many other problems, depression is easier to treat when it's diagnosed early.

DISORIENTATION OR CONFUSION

After the Twin Towers collapsed in New York City on September 11, 2001, survivors were found wandering about in apparent shock, confused and disoriented. Some could not remember where they lived, or where they had come from. Others could not even tell rescue workers their names. These emotions are common in the wake of extremely traumatic events—but they also can occur in less dramatic situations, such as the situation described below.

When Shakia suddenly broke up with Brendon after four years of dating, Brendon didn't know what to think or to do. For days he wandered about, distracted and disoriented. He couldn't concentrate. He couldn't sleep. He'd find himself standing in the bathroom, looking at himself in the mirror and hardly recognizing who he was. He had no interest in his schoolwork, his friends, or his family. He simply couldn't get his head around the fact that his relationship with Shakia was over.

In time, Brendon accepted that he and Shakia were through and he moved on, once again able to enjoy his family, friends, and activities.

While confusion and disorientation are common emotional responses to extreme stress, they also can be caused by certain medical or psychological conditions, excessive alcohol or drug use, side effects of certain prescription drugs, and for other reasons.

COPING WITH EMOTIONAL RESPONSES TO STRESS

The emotional responses to stress described above are normal and common; they usually lessen over time and eventually disappear. Sometimes, however, emotional effects do not disappear on their own.

Someone who has been physically or sexually abused, for instance, may continue to experience emotional effects from the abuse, even after the abuser has been put in jail, or moved away, or died. People who live through disasters such as floods or hurricanes, who are involved either as civilians or soldiers in wars, or who witness or are victims of violence sometimes experience the emotional effects for many years in the form of post-traumatic stress disorder or another anxiety disorder. Even an event such as a car accident or being attacked by a dog can result in lasting emotional effects.

Just as experiencing the effects of stress on a constant basis or over a long period of time can affect your physical health, long-term exposure to the emotional effects of stress can negatively affect your mental health. Learning how to deal with the effects of stress and to manage your stress and your stressors is very important in maintaining both physical and emotional health.

WHAT YOU NEED TO KNOW

- ▸ Emotional response to stress can be immediate and very strong.
- ▸ Common emotional responses to stress include fear and anxiety, anger and irritability, depression, a sense of failure, aggression or withdrawn behavior, and confusion and disorientation.
- ▸ People experience different emotional responses to stress and will behave differently as a result.

➤ Just as long-term or chronic stress can cause physical problems, emotional problems can result as well, and can continue long after the source of the stress has stopped, sometimes in the form of post-traumatic stress disorder.

➤ Learning to manage your responses to stress is important for your long-term health.

6 |||

Long-term Physical Effects of Stress

You read in chapter 4 about the physical responses our bodies have to stress, the physiological reasons for those changes, and how those responses have helped humans to survive and evolve over thousands of years.

It's ironic that while stress has helped humans over the years to escape from or confront dangerous or difficult situations, it has actually developed the potential to become a dangerous situation in itself. That's because, instead of kicking in when a high-stress situation occurs and then relaxing when the stress passes, the stress response systems in many people remain active almost constantly. In such cases, the body is exposed to high amounts of cortisol and other stress hormones, which can be physically harmful over time and contribute to a variety of problems.

So you can see that, while short-term stress can be useful and necessary, long-term, prolonged, or unrelenting stress is not a good thing. What begins as a nervous stomach or feelings of nausea during a short-term stressful situation can develop into irritable bowel syndrome, ulcers, and other serious physical ailments in cases in which stress is constant and severe.

The American Academy of Pediatrics has already warned that more and more teens are exhibiting physical symptoms linked to stress, including headaches, chest pain, sleep disorders, and belly pain. That's worrisome news, since those sorts of problems have the potential to become more serious and result in conditions such as digestive disorders, sleeping disorders, migraines, heart disease, and perhaps even contribute to some types of cancer. Doctors are urging their patients to be aware of the warning signs of stress-related physical problems and to take measures to address them.

In this chapter we'll have a look at situations that can result in long-term stress, how long-term stress can affect you physically, what physical symptoms you might experience, and how you can recognize potential problems. Long-term stress also can have significant psychological effects, and you'll learn more about those in the next chapter. To begin, let's look at some common and not-so-common situations that can result in continual or frequent stress.

WHY AM I ALWAYS STRESSED OUT?

As you know from previous chapters, some people are more susceptible to stress than others, and some are better able to deal with it when it occurs. Some situations, however, are pretty much universally stressful, as noted on the Holmes and Rahe stress scale. Among those universal stressors are the deaths of a spouse or child, divorce or separation, serving time in jail, death of a family member, illness, marriage, pregnancy, a child leaving home, changing schools, and having a mortgage. (It's interesting that even occasions or events that we consider to be happy ones—such as getting married or preparing to welcome a new baby into the family—come to us with a good measure of stress).

Fortunately, most of these big stressors occur only on an occasional basis and are not ongoing. Some situations, though, are ongoing and can result in ongoing or constant stress.

Certainly, ongoing physical, sexual, or emotional abuse is reason for extreme levels of stress. So is living in a violent environment, such as a war zone or even a very dangerous urban neighborhood. These sorts of situations, even if they stop, have long-lasting results, including both physical and psychological problems.

While it's impossible to ignore terribly traumatic experiences like physical, sexual, or emotional abuse or other forms of violence, there are other stressors that might be so constant in your life that you don't even recognize them. It's a worrisome fact that you can get accustomed to living with stressful situations to the point where you barely think about them—they're just the way it is. These situations might include constant worrying about succeeding in school, getting accepted into college, finding the money to go to college or rent an apartment, getting invited to the prom this year, your girlfriend or boyfriend breaking up with you—these sorts of low-level stressors that often remain under the radar. They might not be at the forefront of your mind's agenda, but they're always a little below the surface, nagging at you like a mosquito bite that won't stop itching.

PHYSICAL SYMPTOMS OF ONGOING STRESS

If you're exposed to ongoing or long-term stress, you might notice over time that your neck and shoulders feel cramped and tight, making it difficult some days to even turn your head without neck pain. You might notice that your stomach is frequently churning, and you wonder if it's safe to eat or whether you should skip lunch and just have a soda. You don't understand why you have headaches so often until your dentist says she can tell that you've been grinding your teeth as you sleep, a habit that often results in headaches. To top

---

A Checklist of Stress-Related Physical Symptoms

If you are experiencing any of these symptoms on a regular basis, you may be at danger for long-term physical problems. Use this checklist to determine if you're at risk.

☐ Tightness in the chest

☐ Backache

☐ Sore shoulders and/or neck

☐ Twitching muscles

☐ Feeling out of breath for no reason

☐ Excessive sweating

☐ Muscle twitching

☐ Nausea

☐ Fatigue

☐ Frequent colds

☐ Rashes

☐ Changes in menstrual cycle

☐ Headaches or migraines

☐ Increased allergies

☐ Sudden onset of allergies

☐ Fainting

☐ Decreased sex drive

☐ Sudden weight loss or gain

☐ Indigestion

☐ Stomach cramps

it off, your asthma, which you thought you'd outgrown by sixth or seventh grade, has returned, making it difficult for you to play on the baseball team.

You feel like your body is falling apart and you're only 18 years old! What will it be like when you're 40 or 50 or 60? If you feel that you're stressed out and already experiencing some physical problems as a result, the best thing you can do is to address the situation now. If you don't learn how to handle stressful situations now can mean that you'll lack the skills you need to cope with them as you get older, and it's likely that physical problems would only become more severe. Let's take a look at some of the serious physical conditions that are associated with stress, and the problems they can cause.

STRESS AND HIGH BLOOD PRESSURE

Also known as hypertension, high blood pressure causes the heart to work harder to pump blood to the body and contributes to cardiovascular disease, stroke, eye problems, and kidney disease. While experts are still trying to determine whether long-term stress actually causes high blood pressure, evidence strongly points to a connection between the two. The School of Public Health at Johns Hopkins University in Baltimore reported on a study which revealed that ongoing stress among teens can lead to elevated blood pressure, more than doubling the risk that those teens would experience chronic high blood pressure as adults.

Increasing numbers of teens also are experiencing elevated blood pressure levels due to factors such as obesity, inactivity, and poor eating habits. Other factors that contribute to high blood pressure include genetics and aging. High blood pressure has been called "the silent killer," because there usually are no symptoms. This makes the condition particularly dangerous.

A doctor or nurse can measure your blood pressure with a device called a sphygmomanometer, which consists of a stethoscope, arm cuff, dial, pump, and valve. You can also get your blood pressure taken at health fairs, at special machines in some drug or grocery stores, or with home blood pressure monitors. High blood pressure can be treated with lifestyle changes and medications, if necessary. People who are susceptible to hypertension should be careful to monitor their blood pressure so it can be kept at an acceptable level. If you've never had your blood pressure taken, or haven't had it taken for a long time, it's a good idea to do so in order to establish a baseline reading. If you have your blood pressure taken several times with similar results, you'll be able to keep an eye on it to see if remains about the same.

Keep in mind, though, that blood pressure is susceptible to your reactions to what's going on around you and can vary significantly within a short period of time. If you're on your way to a health fair to have your blood pressure checked and you're nearly run over by a bus on your way, for instance, chances are your blood pressure will be quite high when you arrive! A good thing to do would be to wait for an hour or two and have it taken again to see if it's come down.

Blood pressure for some people tends to elevate just at the thought of having it checked, resulting in a sort of false reading. Some people with high blood pressure do well to purchase a machine they can use at home to keep track of daily readings. If there's a history of high blood pressure in your family—that is, if your mom, dad, or any of your grandparents have or had the condition—you should get yours checked occasionally and keep track of the results.

STRESS AND HEART DISEASE

As with high blood pressure, it's not yet clear whether stress is an independent factor or a primary cause of heart disease, but evidence strongly points to a link. It's sort of like a chain, where one link leads to another. People who are under a lot of stress for a prolonged period might end up feeling isolated or angry, traits which have been linked to increased risk of heart disease. Or, stress causes some people to react with unhealthy behaviors, such as smoking, excessive drinking, physical inactivity, or overeating, all of which also can contribute to heart disease. Experts suspect that high stress levels can further elevate blood pressure and levels of cholesterol, which is a soft, waxy substance found in your body's bloodstream and cells. Everyone needs cholesterol, but when too much of it builds up it can block the flow of blood to the heart and result in health problems, including heart attack. Some studies suggest that stress changes the way the blood clots, and that could be a factor for heart disease. If stress actually is a primary factor in heart disease, it could be due to frequent and excessive exposure to stress-related hormones such as cortisol and adrenaline.

Regardless of whether stress is a cause or a contributor to heart disease, the evidence certainly points to a link between the two.

The term *heart disease* actually refers to a number of conditions that affect the heart, including coronary heart disease and heart attack, congestive heart failure, and congenital heart disease. Together, those conditions cause more than 652,000 deaths in the

United States every year, according to the Centers for Disease Control and Prevention—more than any other disease. The most common type of heart disease is coronary heart disease, which is when the arteries that allow blood to flow to and from the heart get narrowed and hardened due to buildup of plaque.

Some people don't have any symptoms of coronary heart disease until they have a heart attack, also known as a myocardial infarction. This happens when the heart can't get enough blood and the cells of the heart muscle don't receive enough oxygen and begin to die. The more time that passes between the beginning of a heart attack and the start of treatment to restore blood flow, the more damage will occur to the heart muscle. If the heart sustains a great deal of damage, cardiac arrest could result; this is when the heartbeat stops, and it can lead to death.

Other people get a warning that coronary heart disease is present in the form of angina, which is a pain or feeling of pressure in the chest, and sometimes in the shoulders, arms, and back. This occurs when the heart muscle isn't receiving enough oxygen.

Tests to determine whether or not a patient suffers from coronary heart disease include:

- Electrocardiogram (EKG), which measures the electrical rhythms, rate, and regularity of the heartbeat
- Echocardiogram, which provides an image of the heart
- Exercise stress test, which measures how effectively the heart pumps when it's working harder than usual, requiring more oxygen for the heart muscle
- Chest X-ray, which provides an image of the inside of the chest, including the heart
- Cardiac catheterization, in which a thin tube is inserted into an artery in the groin or arm and threaded up to reach the coronary arteries. This allows a doctor to check the insides of coronary arteries to determine blockage and other factors affecting the arteries and your heart.
- Coronary angiography, which is when a dye is injected through the catheter used in a cardiac catheterization, allowing a doctor a better look at the flow of blood and whether blockages are present

Treatment for coronary heart disease usually involves making lifestyle changes, and it often includes medicines and medical treatments. Sometimes, but not always, surgery is required to open arteries and improve blood flow.

Congestive heart failure, sometimes called chronic heart failure, occurs when the heart can't pump enough blood and oxygen to keep other body organs healthy and functioning properly. This can result in a number of serious problems, including kidney failure and other conditions. There is no cure for congestive heart failure, but in many cases it can be managed through lifestyle and with medicines and other treatments.

Congenital heart disease is the most common type of major birth defect; it can be caused by genetic factors, or, sometimes, because a developing fetus is exposed to something that damages the heart. Congenital heart defects include abnormal valves and holes in the walls that divide the chambers of the heart.

Simply being exposed to high levels of stress does not cause any of these conditions. In people who have other risk factors or existing problems, however, stress is suspected as a contributing factor to heart disease.

STRESS AND STROKES

Strokes are sometimes called "brain attacks" because, as during a heart attack, blood flow is restricted. With a stroke, however, the blood flow to the brain is cut off, meaning that the brain doesn't get the oxygen and glucose that it needs to survive, and brain cells begin to die. If a stroke is not treated early, it can cause permanent brain damage.

There are two kinds of stroke: ischemic and hemorrhagic. Ischemic stroke, which accounts for about 80 percent of all strokes, occurs because either a blood clot or too much plaque clogs blood vessels and blocks the flow of blood to the brain. A hemorrhagic stroke occurs when a blood vessel in the brain breaks or ruptures and blood seeps into brain tissue, damaging brain cells.

Although stress does not directly cause strokes to occur, people with high blood pressure are four to six times as likely to have a stroke as those who don't have high blood pressure, and stress also has been connected to other risk factors for stroke, including irregular heart rhythm, smoking, excessive use of alcohol, being overweight, and coronary artery disease.

STRESS AND THE IMMUNE SYSTEM

The immune system is an amazing collection of cells, proteins, tissues, and organs that continually work together to fight off substances that threaten to harm the human body. The immune system employs a series of steps, known collectively as the immune response, to seek out and destroy organisms and substances that, if left alone, could cause disease or infection. When the immune system is functioning properly, it is incredibly effective in protecting you. It can kill bacteria, viruses, and infected cells; assure immunity from diseases; and generally help keep you healthy.

When the immune system is compromised, or not working properly, however, it is not always able to protect the body as it should. Basically, there are four things that go wrong with the immune system: immunodeficiency disorder, autoimmune disorder, allergic disorder, and cancers of the immune system.

Immunodeficiency disorder occurs when parts of the immune system are not working the way they should—or don't even exist. Some people are born with deficient immune systems, while the immune systems of others are damaged by infections or drugs. There are different levels of immunodeficiency disorder, ranging from mild to severe. People with mild immunodeficiency disorders might suffer from allergies and tend to get more colds and other respiratory infections than others, while someone with very severe immunodeficiency disorder may be almost completely helpless in fighting infection. You may have heard of "the bubble boy disease," a condition called severe combined immunodeficiency. Its more informal name comes from the case of a boy from Texas who lived in a plastic bubble that had to be kept entirely free of germs because his damaged immune system did not allow him to fight off any sort of infection. That, of course, is an extreme form of immunodeficiency disorder.

Sometimes immunodeficiency disorder occurs when the immune system is damaged by a disease or certain types of drugs. AIDS (acquired immunodeficiency syndrome) is a disease that, over time, destroys the immune system by making it unable to fight off what would normally be harmless organisms. Some medicines, including chemotherapy and immunosuppressant medicines given to people who have had organ transplants, also can cause immunodeficiency disorder.

Autoimmune disorders occur when something in the immune system goes haywire, causing it to attack a part of the body as if it were an invader looking to cause harm. Autoimmune disorders include lupus, which causes pain in the joints and muscles and can involve the kidneys and other organs; juvenile rheumatoid arthritis, in which the immune system attacks joints of the hands, feet, or knees; and scleroderma, which leads to inflammation of the skin, internal organs and joints. These disorders can be life altering and debilitating.

Sometimes the immune system overreacts to certain substances within the body, causing an allergic disorder. This can cause symptoms ranging from sneezing and watery eyes to a dangerous condition called anaphylaxis. Examples of allergic disorders include asthma; eczema; drug allergies; seasonal allergies; food allergies; animal allergies; allergies to toxins, such as bee stings; and environmental allergies, such as allergies to dust mites or mold.

Cancers can occur in the immune system, as in other parts of the body, when cells grow in an uncontrolled manner. This damages the immune system and makes it unable to do its work. The two most common types of cancers affecting kids and teenagers are leukemia and lymphoma. Thankfully, most cases of these cancers are curable.

Researchers and doctors have discovered a link between stress and disorders of the immune system. Studies have shown that long-term stress, particularly when those experiencing it can not see any ending to it or have no hope of escaping it, weakens almost all aspects of the immune system, making those affected more susceptible to a variety of problems. Some researchers believe this is due to the presence of cortisol, a stress-related hormone that may affect the cells within the immune system and limit their ability to fight off diseases.

Continued research is occurring as scientists and doctors learn more about the ways in which stress affects the immune system. It has been observed, however, that people exposed to long-term stress are more susceptible to a variety of problems, ranging from colds to cancer. Addressing overall health is extremely important when considering the immune system and how to keep it at peak functioning levels. Proper nutrition, sufficient exercise, and keeping stress under control are all factors that affect how efficiently your immune system works.

CAN STRESS CAUSE CANCER?

There is no proof that stress, by itself, causes cancer. Studies conducted over the past three decades, however, have suggested a relationship between psychological factors, including stress, and cancer risk, according to the National Cancer Institutes, a branch of the National Institutes of Health.

While some studies have indicated that stress might actually increase the risk of developing cancer, others have suggested that high stress levels may lead to faster progression of the disease once it occurs. Still other studies have linked stress to certain types of virus-related tumors that occur when the immune system is compromised.

This is a complicated topic, because, as with high blood pressure and heart disease, it's not known whether stress is a factor in the development of cancer, or if it contributes to the effects of other cancer factors, such as obesity, smoking, and alcohol abuse. Someone with a strong family history of cancer may experience a great deal of stress worrying that she too will get cancer, raising the question of whether the stress may contribute to the likelihood of the cancer occurring. And, researchers wonder, once cancer has been diagnosed, could the stress that accompanies such a diagnoses contribute to the progression of the disease?

Most scientists believe that cancer is caused by a combination of factors, including genetics and environmental and behavioral factors. As more research is conducted, we should get a better understanding of a possible link between stress and cancer. We do know, however, that stress can negatively affect the immune system, and the immune system is an important tool in fending off cancer.

STRESS AND OBESITY

A common stress response for many people is to eat. And, generally, when you're feeling stressed out and looking for relief, a celery stalk is not the first food you reach for. Most people who seek stress relief through food gravitate toward foods high in fat, sugar, and salt—pizza, fried chicken, and donuts, rather than fruits, vegetables, and whole grains.

Many people eat when they are bored, happy, sad, angry, or frustrated—not just because they are hungry. Researcher Brian Wansink claims that the average person makes about 200 decisions pertaining to food every day, most of which are made with little thought or awareness, and most of which have hardly anything to do with hunger. Eating habits, Wansink asserts, depend largely on who we're with, where we are, and how we're feeling at the time we decide to eat. So, if you and friend always take a different route home from school on Fridays because you stop at the café for a water ice or gelato, you're likely to indulge, even if you're not particularly hungry. If you're feeling stressed or upset, you might indulge even more than you normally would.

There's a lot of truth to jokey mottoes such as "When all else goes wrong, reach for chocolate," because that's exactly what many people do. Some people use food for escape, just as others might use alcohol or drugs.

A recently released study of more than 1,000 low-income adolescents in Boston, San Antonio, and Chicago revealed that kids who reported high levels of stress based on five factors experienced an obesity rate almost 10 percent higher than their peers who did not feel overly stressed. The five factors considered were: academic problems, drug or alcohol use, depression or poor mental health, aggressive behavior, and lack of future orientation.

The increased obesity in the highly stressed kids could be caused by behaviors adopted in response to stress, such as overeating and not exercising, researchers said. Or, obesity itself may be a stressor, leading to a vicious cycle.

In addition to stress-affected eating habits, scientists recently discovered another connection between stress and weight gain. A study led by Georgetown University Medical Center revealed that a molecule called neuropeptide Y (NPY), which helps in new tissue growth, is released from certain nerve cells during times of stress. The NPY molecule has been linked to appetite and obesity, leading researchers to suspect a link between stress and fat growth. The body of a person who experiences stressful situations on a regular basis could be releasing this molecule often, promoting the production of fat.

STRESS AND DIABETES

Diabetes is another disease which, although not caused by stress, may be affected by it. And, stress may be a contributing factor in the presence of the disease. When someone has diabetes, his or her body doesn't produce insulin (type 1 diabetes), or doesn't use insulin properly (type 2 diabetes). Insulin is a hormone necessary to convert sugar, starches, and other foods into energy. Nearly 8 percent of the American population has diabetes, and the incidence of the disease is rising. Both genetics and environmental factors, including obesity, play a role in the development of this disease.

Ninety to 95 percent of people suffering from diabetes have type 2, in which their bodies don't use insulin properly. Traditionally, type 2 was known as "adult diabetes," because it usually didn't occur until well into adulthood. Today, however, children as young as seven have been found to exhibit early signs of type 2 diabetes, and, alarmingly, the number of children being diagnosed with this type of the disease is increasingly rapidly. Overall, the incidence of diabetes in the United States increased by 13.5 percent between 2005 and 2007, according to the American Diabetes Association.

Experiencing frequent stress poses particular problems for someone with diabetes. When the fight-or-flight response kicks in, so do stress hormones. The hormones allow stored up energy in the body to be released into the cells to get the body into shape for fleeing or fighting. A person who has diabetes may not have insulin to help that stored-up energy get into the cells—the glucose and fat that makes up the energy gets stacked up in the blood. For such a person, stress occurring on a regular or constant basis, can result in long periods of high levels of glucose in the blood.

Also, people who have diabetes and find themselves under stress may not take care of themselves as well as they should, which can have a negative effect on their health.

As you have read, long-term stress plays a role in a number of very serious diseases, as well as causing less serious problems such as headaches, digestive problems, neck and shoulder pain, sleeping problems, and skin rashes. If you are already experiencing any of the physical problems associated with stress, you should make an appointment to see your doctor. If you haven't had a physical examination for two years or more, it's advisable to try to schedule one. If you don't have a family doctor or can't afford to see a doctor, there may be alternatives available to you. You'll read more about that in chapter 11, "Paying for Care."

WHAT YOU NEED TO KNOW

➤ While short-term stress can be useful, long-term stress can cause a variety of problems, including serious physical conditions.

➤ Many people become accustomed to living with ongoing stress and no longer recognize that the stressful situation exists.

➤ If you're already experiencing physical symptoms of stress, you should address the situation now so it doesn't continue to worsen as you get older.

➤ Stress is believed to play a role in high blood pressure, heart disease, stroke, problems of the immune system, cancer, obesity, and diabetes.

➤ While stress doesn't cause these serious diseases and conditions, it might contribute to their presence or make them worse once they are diagnosed.

➤ If you believe you may be experiencing stress-related physical problems, you should consult with a doctor or other health professional.

7 ▋▋▋

Long-term Psychological Effects of Stress

Just as long-term exposure to stress can contribute to physical problems, it also can have profound psychological effects. Too much stress over time can negatively affect your brain, particularly your memory. It also can affect your ability to concentrate and make good decisions, and contribute to anxiety, depression, and other psychological disorders.

These psychological issues can contribute to a host of other problems, ranging from substance abuse to aggression and violence.

As a quick review, remember that psychological stress is stress that comes from within, often caused by expectations we set for ourselves, or the expectations from others that we internalize. It also can result from messages that others give us. If someone tells you when you're young, either by words or actions, that you're ugly or worthless or stupid, you're likely to internalize those messages and carry them with you. This creates ongoing emotional or psychological stress over time, which can have negative consequences.

It doesn't always take years, however, for emotional stress to result in symptoms. The Centers for Disease Control and Prevention (CDC) lists emotional responses that commonly occur following a traumatic or otherwise stressful event. The responses can include: anxiety, guilt, grief, denial, panic, fear, anger or irritability, loss of emotional control, depression, sense of failure, feeling overwhelmed, blaming others or oneself. Some of these reactions usually are short-term responses to emotional stress, while others, such as depression, can be long-term responses. Some responses, such as anger, can occur in the short term, and then remain for a long time after the cause of stress has stopped.

Let's look at some examples of how psychological stress occurs, and then we'll examine some of the long-term consequences that can result from that stress.

UNREALISTIC AND UNATTAINABLE EXPECTATIONS

It may be that for some reason you expect that you should always be in control, you get the best grades of anyone in your class, be able to participate in numerous after school activities, hold down a part-time job, spend every weekend at baseball tournaments, and be the go-to person for every friend who runs into a problem, all the while holding it together for yourself and everyone around you.

Or, it may be that you don't see yourself as that person at all, but your parents do, and they've made sure since the time you were four years old that you knew it. You feel forced to try to live up to their unrealistic expectations at the cost of feeling, some days, like you could actually explode. Unrealistic expectations can also come from peer pressure and societal pressures, by telling you that you have to look, act, and behave in a certain manner.

Living with unrealistic expectations, whether placed on you by yourself or someone else, is a common source of psychological stress, and can result in short- and long-term problems.

SELF-ESTEEM

Poor self-esteem often can be a huge source of psychological stress. Remember the story in chapter 3 about Jennifer, who in fifth grade experienced an early growth spurt and for a short time was the biggest kid in her class? Even after the other kids caught up with her, she couldn't get over her conviction that she was huge and misshapen and her body was horrible. Jennifer has suffered from years from a distorted body image, resulting in very poor self-esteem, which has been devastating for her.

A consequence of this warped self-perception of her appearance is that Jennifer closely monitors everything she eats. She counts calories and obsesses about food ingredients, fat content, fiber, and carbohydrates. Recently, she has resorted to purging as a means of controlling her weight. A difficult piece of the puzzle with Jennifer is that her friends and family have a hard time understanding her obsession with her size, because she looks quite normal. Despite therapy, Jennifer has a ways to go in reconciling her body image and relieving herself of the psychological stress she has suffered from for years.

Self-esteem issues can result from other situations, as well, and come from a variety of sources. A parent telling an adolescent that she's too heavy can result in damaged self-esteem, as can getting cut from the basketball team, a breakup with a boyfriend or girlfriend, or any of variety of other situations. Self-esteem issues can be short term, or cause problems into adulthood, depending on their severity and how they are handled.

ABUSE

It's hard to imagine someone hurting a child, but Sonya was abused sexually by her mother's boyfriend, who later became her stepfather, from the time she was six years old until she was 13, and finally told a teacher at her school. Sonya learned at an early age how to make herself small, to avoid even looking at other people, and to stay out of the way, but she couldn't avoid the abuse that went on for years, even after she told her mother about it. She suffered great psychological stress over a long period of time, causing great harm not only in the short term, but possibly for the rest of her life.

Abuse is not limited to sexual abuse, but can be physical or emotional, as well. Neglect also is a form of abuse. And it's important to understand that not all abuse is intentional. Some parents or other caregivers are simply incapable of caring for their children, which can result in physical, emotional, and other sorts of problems. Unfortunately, problems of abused children too often get passed along to their own children, resulting in a cycle of abuse.

OTHER DANGERS OR VIOLENCE

Most people occasionally encounter a dangerous situation or are exposed to some sort of violence. You might find yourself stuck outside in a thunderstorm, with lightning flashing around you and no source of shelter. You might be involved in a car crash, or witness a crime, or even be the victim of a crime. You might have a close call while crossing a busy street and almost get struck by a car. You could fall off a horse, or off a ladder, or off a balance beam. Life is filled with potentially hazardous experiences. Some people, however, are exposed to danger and violence on a regular basis, which can be emotionally devastating with far-reaching results.

Quentin was the oldest of three children of a single mom living in Brooklyn, New York. His mom tried hard, working two jobs to support her children. She was rarely home, forcing the kids to pretty much raise themselves, and they never had enough money. When he was 14, Quentin started selling drugs on the street to earn money for the family. Against his mother's wishes, he dropped out of high school when he was in ninth grade and began dealing drugs full-time. Soon, he'd joined a gang.

Quentin knew this lifestyle was plenty dangerous, and he experienced a lot of stress in the form of fear. He witnessed a lot of violence, as did his siblings and mother, who not only worried for themselves, but that Quentin would be hurt or killed. One night Quentin was shot in the leg during a fight with a rival gang. His injury wasn't life threatening, and, in fact, may have saved his life, since his mother then decided to move to a city in Pennsylvania in hopes of keeping her family safe. Quentin eventually went back to high school and graduated, and plans to go on to college and get a counseling degree so he can help others. Still, he suffers emotionally from the long-term effects of the stress he experienced.

LONG-TERM PSYCHOLOGICAL EFFECTS OF STRESS

It's important to understand that long-term stress can cause physical and psychological problems that occur together. Sometimes it's difficult to tell which comes first, and if one contributes to the other. In the last chapter, for instance, you read that long-term stress is thought to be a factor in high blood pressure, heart disease, stroke, obesity, problems with the immune system, some cancers, and diabetes. And you read earlier that poor health is a major cause of stress and can lead to anxiety, depression, and other problems, all of which can be the effects of long-term psychological stress. So you see, the causes and effects of long-term physical and psychological stress are closely tied together. Let's look at some of the conditions that can result from long-term psychological stress.

STRESS AND ANXIETY DISORDERS

As with some of the physical problems associated with long-term stress, it's not clear if anxiety disorders are actually caused by stress, but it is clear that the two are linked. Anxiety disorders often become exacerbated when someone is under a lot of stress, and disorders can trigger the onset of an anxiety disorder.

Anxiety disorders are common, affecting as many as one out of every eight teenagers. They are, in fact, the most common mental health condition in America. Generally, there are six kinds of anxiety disorders. It can be hard to diagnose a specific disorder, because many of the symptoms are the same. General symptoms of an anxiety disorder include: feelings of panic and fear; uncontrollable, obsessive thoughts; repeated thoughts or flashbacks of a traumatic experience; nightmares and sleeping problems; cold or sweaty hands and/or feet; ritualistic behaviors, such as repeatedly washing your hands or constantly playing with your hair; shortness of breath; heart palpitations; dry mouth; being unable to be still and calm; numbness or tingling in the hands or feet; muscle tension; dizziness; and nausea.

All anxiety disorders share the common symptom of excessive fear that occurs when there's no real reason for it. If a dog is running at you growling and snarling, for example, that's reason to be fearful, and you will experience physical and emotional responses to that fear. If you see a dog on a leash in the park, however, and you experience the same type of fear, that's anxiety. You know that the dog on the leash doesn't pose a threat to you because it's under control and looks perfectly friendly, but you still experience the responses. There are six types of anxiety disorder:

Generalized anxiety disorder (GAD). This disorder results in constant worry about nearly everything. You may always expect the worst to happen, even though there's no reason to do so. GAD also can cause physical symptoms such as fatigue, headaches, nausea, or muscle tension.

Social phobia. Also called social anxiety disorder, this condition causes an overwhelming fear of being embarrassed or humiliated in a social situation. People with social phobias sometimes avoid going out at all because they dread attention. As you can imagine, this can be very debilitating, because it can keep you away from activities and situations that could be very worthwhile and/or enjoyable.

Post-traumatic stress disorder (PTSD). PTSD sometimes occurs after a traumatic event such as being the victim of a crime, a car accident, a natural disaster, or an unprecedented incident such as 9/11. Symptoms can include irritability; nightmares; flashbacks; anger; depression; and a feeling of being numb or lacking emotions. Sufferers of PTSD also may feel an overwhelming need to avoid anything that reminds them of the incident. This can be disruptive not only to the person with PTSD, but to friends and family members as well.

Panic disorder. Someone with panic disorder experiences feelings of extreme fear or terror that occur suddenly and repeatedly, without any warning. These experiences, often called panic attacks, can include symptoms such as sweating, chest pain, irregular heartbeat, and breathing problems. Panic attacks are particularly distressing, and people with panic disorder sometimes resist going out because they fear an attack will occur. People who suffer from panic attacks sometimes fear that they're dying or losing their minds.

Obsessive-compulsive disorder (OCD). OCD involves repeated, unwanted thoughts that result in compulsive behaviors such as constant hand washing or showering, checking things over and over, such as making sure the stove is turned off or the door is locked; arranging objects in a very particular manner; repeating a name or phrase over and over; holding onto unnecessary items such as junk mail or old newspapers; and constant counting of specific objects. Someone who has OCD may be aware of such behavior, but feels unable to stop engaging in it.

Specific phobias. Someone with a specific phobia has a terrible fear of something that is not likely to cause any danger or is not a common presence in his or her life. Someone can be desperately afraid of spiders, for example, even if he or she rarely even sees spiders and has ever been bitten by one.

Anxiety disorders can be extremely distressing, and they are serious conditions, but they are treatable. Often, other mental health conditions, such as depression, accompany an anxiety disorder, along with behaviors such as eating disorders or substance abuse. The cause of anxiety disorders isn't entirely clear, but they may be caused by chemical imbalances within the body, to which long-term stress may be a contributor. There also appears to be a genetic component to anxiety disorders.

STRESS AND DEPRESSION

Jamie appeared to have everything going for her: She had a lot of friends, was a terrific softball player, active in her church youth group, and worked hard and earned good grades in school. She was generally a happy teenager with relatively few problems and an optimistic future.

Over a period of time, however, Jamie began to feel tired and sort of irritable. Her friends seemed annoying with their little jokes, giggling, and secrets. Even softball got to be more of a pain than the

Stress and the Brain

The same beneficial processes that occur in the brain during periods of short-term stress may be detrimental in the long run, researchers have found. A stressful event causes the body to experience a rush of adrenaline, during which time the part of the brain called the adrenal cortex releases hormones and chemicals called glucocoticoids, or GCs. GCs are helpful in dealing with stressful situation in which you need to think and react quickly. They tell your brain to either rev up and increase its awareness, or to slow down. They also help us to remember stressful events, making it easier to handle similar events should they occur again.

So, while GCs can be beneficial, they can actually damage or even kill the sensitive neurons (cells) of the brain if they are present on an ongoing basis, as with chronic stress. In particular, GCs can affect the part of the brain that controls memory.

great time it had been before, and Jamie felt like she just didn't have the energy to do it anymore. Every chance she got, Jamie would crawl into her bed and take a nap, and it seemed like it was getting harder and harder to get back out.

Jamie knew her parents were worried about her, and that made her feel bad, but she couldn't help how she was feeling. Her dad kept telling her to pull herself together, and she wished, more than anything, that she could. She started feeling guilty that she felt so bad, because she couldn't think of any specific problem or situation that would cause her to feel so sad. Her friends began drifting away, and Jamie couldn't find the energy to keep in touch with them. She felt more and more alone, which made her feel even more sad and hopeless. One day she completely broke down and told her mom that she couldn't take it anymore. Frightened about what was happening to her daughter, Jamie's mom made an appointment with the family doctor, who suspected Jamie was suffering from depression and referred her to a therapist.

Jamie didn't experience any particular event that triggered her depression, but she became depressed, regardless. While there certainly is a link between stress and depression, most experts agree that major depression, also known as depressive disorder or clinical depression, is caused by a combination of brain chemistry, genetics, and your emotional environment. Other factors that can contribute to depression include illness, diet, medications, and substance abuse.

The National Institute of Mental Health describes depression as "when the blues don't go away," and lists 11 common symptoms:

➤ Ongoing sad, anxious, or empty feelings
➤ Feelings of hopelessness
➤ Feelings of guilt, worthlessness, or helplessness
➤ Feeling irritable or restless
➤ Loss of interest in activities or hobbies that were once enjoyable, including sex
➤ Feeling tired all the time
➤ Difficulty concentrating, remembering details, or difficulty making decisions
➤ Being unable to go to sleep or stay asleep (insomnia); waking in the middle of the night, or sleeping all the time
➤ Overeating or loss of appetite
➤ Thoughts of suicide or making suicide attempts
➤ Ongoing aches and pains, headaches, cramps or digestive problems that do not go away

About 19 million people experience depression every year, according to the National Institutes of Health, and the majority of those people don't receive the help they need. Depression affects people of both sexes and of every race, ethnic background, and socioeconomic group. If you are experiencing some, or all, of these symptoms and you believe you are suffering from depression, it's very important that you discuss your situation with a parent, the school nurse, your doctor, a community counselor, or another trusted adult who will assist you in getting help.

We don't fully understand why some people become depressed while others don't. There's evidence that some types of depression run in families, and that brain chemistry and structure are factors in depression. Environmental and psychological stresses, such as the loss of a loved one, a traumatic event, the loss of a job, and poor relationships with others also are thought to trigger depression in some people, but sometimes depression occurs with no clear triggering event, affecting those, like Jamie, who appear to have everything going for them. When that happens, the depressed person may feel very guilty about his condition, as Jamie did, and may be blamed by others, which can cause the depression to worsen. Anyone suffering from depression should understand that it's not their fault, and the condition is not something to feel guilty about. The smartest thing to do if you believe you're suffering from depression is to ask for professional help. Depression is a serious health issue, but it often can be treated. Don't assume, or let someone else tell you, that how you're feeling is just a "stage" you're going through, or that you can "pull yourself out of it."

STRESS AND SUICIDE

One of the major risks of depression among teens is suicide. Suicide, which is linked to both stress and depression, is the third-leading cause of death among young people between the ages of 15 and 24, and the sixth-leading cause of those between 5 and 14, according to the American Academy of Child & Adolescent Psychiatry. About 32,500 people in the United States commit suicide every year, according to the National Institutes of Health, with a disproportionate number of those being teens and the elderly. It's not known exactly how many suicide attempts occur each year, but it's estimated that for each person who actually commits suicide, between eight and 25 people attempt it.

If you have thoughts of harming yourself, or know someone else who does, it is absolutely imperative that you tell someone who can help. Early symptoms of suicidal thinking are listed by the National Institutes of Health as:

- ▶ Depression
- ▶ Statements or expressions of feelings of guilt
- ▶ Tension or anxiety
- ▶ Nervousness
- ▶ Impulsiveness

Critical signs that a person may be getting ready to make a suicide attempt are:

- ▶ Sudden change in behavior, especially calmness after a period of anxiety
- ▶ Giving away belongings or attempting to settle issues
- ▶ Direct or indirect references to suicide
- ▶ Direct attempts at suicide

If you are considering suicide, ask a family member or friend to help you, and do not leave their presence until you have received professional help. If no one is available to help you, call your doctor or call 911. The National Suicide Prevention Lifeline has a toll-free, 24-hour hotline that is staffed by trained counselors. The number is 1-800-273-TALK. If you believe a friend is considering suicide, don't leave them alone, and call for immediate help.

WHAT YOU NEED TO KNOW

> ➤ Just as long-term stress can cause physical problems, it also can have serious psychological effects.
> ➤ Psychological stress can occur as a result of poor self-esteem, unrealistic expectations from yourself or someone else, abuse, or other sources of danger or violence.
> ➤ Stress has been linked to the serious condition of anxiety disorders, of which there are six different types.
> ➤ Experts believe there is a connection between stress and depression, and that long-term stress can actually result in depression.
> ➤ Extreme or ongoing stress may cause someone with suicidal tendencies to act on those tendencies.

8

Addressing Your Stress Problem with Lifestyle Changes

Life moves quickly, and everyone experiences at least occasional periods of stress. If you feel that your stress level has reached the point where it's negatively affecting your life, however, it's time to address the problem and start working to make some changes to help you reduce your stress. You probably can tell when you're overly stressed because you experience some symptoms, such as headaches or digestive problems. The American Psychological Association provides this list of stress symptoms on its Web site:

- Headaches, muscle tension, neck or back pain
- Upset stomach
- Dry mouth
- Chest pains, rapid heartbeat
- Difficulty falling or staying asleep
- Fatigue
- Loss of appetite or overeating "comfort foods"
- Increased frequency of colds
- Lack of concentration or focus
- Memory problems or forgetfulness
- Jitters
- Irritability
- Short temper
- Anxiety

If you're experiencing a number of these symptoms on a regular basis, you'll need to address your stress level and consider what you might do to reduce your stress or at least be able to deal with it more effectively.

Small lifestyle changes, such as staying away from caffeine and making sure you get some exercise each day, can go a long way toward improving your mood and helping you to feel less stressed out and more able to enjoy life.

Remember that a major reason that teens are so susceptible to stress is that they lack control over many aspects of their lives. Most teenagers don't get to choose where they live or go to school; those things have been determined for you by your parents and their life circumstances. Your parents probably set rules that you're expected to follow, even if you don't agree with them. You might feel boxed in by all your activities, or because you're forced to give up your free time to help care for younger brothers and sisters. Maybe you don't have as much money as some of your friends, or your parents can't afford to buy you the brands of clothing that you'd like. All of these circumstances are pretty much out of your control, and that can become a source of stress in itself, or intensify the effects of other sources of stress in your life.

Taking time to stand back, assess your lifestyle and make even small, positive changes will not only result in an improved sense of well-being, but also can help you to feel that you're more in control of your life. That's empowering, and it can go a long way toward reducing your stress level.

Lifestyle changes involve adding positive, healthy behaviors, *and* eliminating unhealthy behaviors. It's making sure, for example, that you get some exercise every day *and* that you don't dive into the Ben and Jerry's whenever you feel your stress level rising.

There are three levels of stress response: the thoughts you have when you experience stress, the feelings or emotions that arise from those thoughts, and the behaviors or responses that result. The most obvious of those three levels are the behaviors, which can be either positive or negative. Of those three levels of stress response, only the behaviors are observable. If you respond to stress by kicking the trash can, people around you see that. They can't see the stress that caused you to respond with thoughts that made you feel really angry and frustrated—they only see you kick the trash can. If you're looking to reduce or better deal with your stress by making some lifestyle changes, your first step should be to make an assessment of the thoughts and emotions you experience when you experience stress, and the behaviors that you exhibit in response.

ASSESSING YOUR THOUGHTS, EMOTIONS, AND BEHAVIORS

Take a little time to think about how you react when you encounter a stressful situation. What thoughts typically come to your mind? What emotions follow those thoughts? Do you feel angry, sad, or frustrated? And, what behaviors do you exhibit in response to those thoughts and emotions? Hopefully, you're not reacting to stress in unhealthy or inappropriate ways, and, if you are, you'll make the decision to ask someone for some help.

Raising your awareness of how you respond and react to stress can help you to assess your emotions and behaviors, which is an important tool if you're going to attempt to change behaviors to help you better deal with stress.

A good idea is to write down the thoughts, emotions, and behaviors you experience when confronted with a stressful situation. If you can get into the habit of doing this, you may begin to notice some patterns. For instance, you might notice that, on the days that you have to rush home from school because your mom goes to work and you have to baby-sit your little brothers and sister, you feel overwhelmed, anxious, and frustrated. And, that those emotions often lead you to stuff yourself with cookies and soda and whatever else you can find to eat. Being aware of your reactions to stress and the behaviors that result is the first step in getting ready to make positive changes in order to better deal with stressful situations.

UNHEALTHY RESPONSES TO STRESS

Alicia is no stranger to stressful situations. Her brother Josh, who's two years old than she is, has had tons of problems and has been in trouble for about four years now—starting when Alicia was in the sixth grade. Beset by problems with drugs and alcohol, her brother has been arrested, put into rehab, run away from home, and even sent off to one of those wilderness programs for kids who get into trouble.

Nothing seems to help, though, and, as you can imagine, Josh's troubles are a constant source of worry and anxiety for Alicia and her parents. It seems that when her parents aren't yelling at Josh, her mom is crying or they're fighting about how to handle the latest crisis. Alicia pretty much stays in the background and tries to keep out of the way, but the truth is, she's got plenty of problems of her own.

Often, when confronted yet again with a stressful situation, Alicia will get thoughts like "This is just way too much for me to handle" or "It's so unfair that my life is like this all the time." Along with those thoughts, she experiences feelings of being sad, overwhelmed, depressed, frustrated, and angry. When the situation gets really bad, and Alicia feels that she can't stand one more minute of the turmoil around her, she has a secret weapon that she uses to make herself feel better—she cuts herself.

Cutting is the act of intentionally scratching or cutting the skin in order to hurt yourself, and it's a type of self-injury that can be extremely harmful and dangerous. While it can bring some relief to someone who's depressed, anxious, or under great stress, the relief doesn't last and the act of harming yourself can get to be a habit. Alicia knows that cutting is not a healthy or acceptable way of dealing with her stress, but she doesn't know what else to do when things get crazy in her house.

Alicia's reaction to the stress that surrounds her begins with thinking "This is way too much for me to handle" or "It's unfair that my life is like this," and progresses to feeling sad, depressed, angry, frustrated, or overwhelmed. Those thoughts and emotions lead her to engage in the unhealthy behavior of cutting herself in an effort to find some relief from her situation. Other people might react negatively to stressful situations by overeating, using drugs or alcohol, or lashing out at others, all of which are unhealthy behaviors. Let's have a closer look at some of those negative behaviors, and then we'll address some healthy, positive ways to help you deal with stress.

SELF-INJURY

Intentionally injuring oneself through cutting or another action is not an overly common behavior, but, as awareness of such acts has increased, we've learned that surprisingly large numbers of teens have tried it. Girls are more likely to cut themselves than boys, although guys are not immune. Both boys and girls also might engage in other methods of self-injury, such as burning themselves with a lighted match or cigarette, punching themselves, or pulling out hair.

While cutting or another form of self injury might make you feel a little better, at least at first, the relief won't last. Most people who cut don't really want to hurt themselves seriously, but there have been cases in which teens have been badly injured by accidentally slicing across an artery or cutting deeper than they'd intended to. Using an unclean tool to cut can result in infection.

Cutting or otherwise harming yourself is a serious situation that needs to be addressed. If you know someone who is engaging in this behavior, or if you are, the first step is to confide in a responsible adult who you trust, and ask for help. Self-injury is a treatable condition, but it may require professional help.

EMOTIONAL EATING

Eating in response to an emotion—when you feel sad, angry, happy, or bored, rather than because your stomach is rumbling with hunger—is called emotional eating. It's a recognized behavior, and one that most people engage in, at least occasionally.

When you're eating to address an emotion, you typically crave a certain food, such as ice cream or candy, rather than being open to different options. Emotional eating often involves eating more than you know you should, or even more than you really want to eat, because you're eating to fill a need or find relief. Hunger associated with emotional eating usually comes on suddenly, as opposed to physical hunger, which occurs gradually.

If you recognize that you eat when you're angry, bored, happy, or sad, try taking another approach by getting some exercise, getting on Facebook and talking to a friend, listening to some good music, or watching a funny TV show or video. Changing your mood often will help you to get over the desire to eat.

While emotional eating is harmless when it occurs only every now and then, continuously using food to find comfort or relief, or to relieve sadness or anger, is an issue that needs to be addressed. Overeating, particularly if you're not getting lots of exercise, can lead to obesity, a condition related to serious health problems.

Emotional eating also can open the door to eating disorders, which are very serious conditions. About one out of every 100 teenage girls develop anorexia nervosa, an eating disorder characterized by a distorted body image, obsessive fear of gaining weight, and drastically limiting food intake. Anorexia nervosa can cause permanent damage to the heart and other organs; in extreme cases, it results in death.

Bulimia nervosa affects two to three of every 100 teen girls, and is characterized by overeating followed by forced vomiting or purging. If you or someone you know is affected by an eating disorder, the situation needs to be addressed.

DRUG AND ALCOHOL ABUSE

When stress occurs over time or repeatedly, some people turn to drugs or alcohol to help them relax and feel better. This, of course, although common, is a very unhealthy means of dealing with stress, and can lead to both short- and long-term problems. Drug and alcohol use can lead to poor school performance, significant health problems, substance dependency, and other negative consequences. Using drugs and alcohol impairs judgment, which can put you at risk for crime, accidents, unsafe sex, and violence. Alcohol-related car accidents are the leading cause of death among teenagers, and every year, more than 100,000 Americans die of causes related to alcohol abuse.

More than half of all high school seniors admit to having used illegal drugs or alcohol, and, nationwide, more than 17 million people suffer from some sort of addiction.

Many teens who experiment with drugs and alcohol as a means of relieving stress think they'll only do it once, or they'll only drink one beer, or they won't ever use any drug except for marijuana. People who are predisposed to addiction, however, can quickly become dependent on drugs and alcohol and find it very difficult, or even impossible, to stop using. When that occurs, lives can be extremely disrupted and relationships destroyed.

Using drugs or alcohol to deal with stress is a very bad idea. If you do not use drugs or alcohol, congratulate yourself and continue to be smart and use good judgment. If you do use drugs or alcohol, or both, get online and read everything you can find about the risks associated. If you're worried that you have a problem with drugs or alcohol, you need to find someone to talk to about your concerns. You should be particularly aware of a potential problem if there's a history of problems with drugs and/or alcohol in your family, for addiction tends to involve genetic components. If you can't talk to a parent for whatever reason, consult with a school nurse, a teacher you trust, a minister or rabbi, or an adult friend who you believe will help you. Getting help with an addiction problem early on can greatly increase the chances of getting you back on track for a happy and productive life. Ignoring a problem with drugs or alcohol now can lead to even bigger problems in the future.

OVERSPENDING

Just as some people eat to relieve stress or fill a void within themselves, other people buy things. This is called compulsive spending, and is a real problem for many people. Researchers estimate that between 2 and 8 percent of Americans are compulsive spenders, some of whom seek treatment for their addictions. Gambling is a form of overspending, and, if it becomes a problem, can involve many of the same characteristics as being addicted to drugs or alcohol.

Compulsive spending is complicated, because, as a society, we're encouraged to spend and buy things we don't need. Companies spend millions of dollars in advertising, hoping to convince us to buy their products.

Overspending can lead to serious financial problems, and result in the same feelings of shame and depression as other addictive behaviors, such as drug use. People who are compulsive spenders have a higher rate of suicide than those who are not. If you consistently buy things you know you don't need, even though you know you should be saving the money you spend for other purposes; or steal money in order to buy things; or feel better about yourself after making some purchases, you might want to talk to a trusted adult about your concerns. You can learn more about compulsive spending at the Debtors Anonymous Web site at www.debtorsanonymous.org.

WITHDRAWAL

Some people react to stressful situations by withdrawing or isolating themselves from others. They find it easier to be alone than to have to explain how they're feeling or deal with others. Some withdraw because they feel sad and don't want to be around others who seem happy.

Some people retreat into video games or virtual worlds, playing for hours or even days on end. Others might read or sleep excessively. While nearly everyone occasionally feels that they need some time alone, shutting out the world isn't a healthy reaction to stress because it doesn't address the issues causing the stress—it merely temporarily removes you from the situation. A better means of coping with stress is to invite a friend to go for a walk and talk about how you're feeling.

AGGRESSION

While some people faced with stressful situations withdraw, others become aggressive and act out. They may express anger and frustration by punching, kicking, or yelling. Some drive aggressively or engage in violent behavior. Aggression can be physical or verbal, and often occurs in the form of bullying. Boys are more likely than girls to practice physical aggression such as shouting at someone or hitting, although the incidence of physical aggression among girls has been increasing. Both girls and boys practice indirect aggression, which includes behaviors such as forming cliques, gossiping, and spreading rumors or lies on the Internet.

Aggression also can be directed toward nonhuman targets. Some people take out their aggression on animals, while others may damage property. Aggressive behavior can cause you to become unpopular and alienated from others, and could even put you at risk for legal and other problems. If you frequently engage in aggressive behavior, you may do well to talk to a counselor or mental-health professional.

COMPULSIVE WORKING OR STUDYING

You've probably heard somebody refer to somebody else as a "workaholic." Just as some people become dependent on alcohol, or shopping, or gambling, others become dependent on working, or, in the case of some teens, doing schoolwork.

People who develop extreme problems with compulsive working sometimes end up losing their families and other important parts of their lives. They find it difficult to think about anything other than work, and become resentful of other areas of life that take them away from work. While work needs to be taken seriously, there's a saying to remember if you ever feel that work is consuming too much of your time and energy: "Your job will never love you back."

FIGHTING BACK AGAINST STRESS WITH POSITIVE BEHAVIORS AND LIFESTYLE CHANGES

Many people engage in unhealthy behaviors when they're overly stressed, but, once you learn to recognize the situations that cause you to feel stressed, you can work to avoid those situations or train yourself to react to them in a more positive manner than by using those behaviors described above. In many cases, you can avoid getting into stressful situations in the first place by getting organized and preparing for what you need to do ahead of time instead of waiting until the last minute. Running around your house looking for your shoes or keys when you know the school bus is coming down the block is a stressful situation, but one that is fully avoidable.

In other instances, it may well be that you can't avoid situations that upset you and cause you to feel stressed out. You might live in a neighborhood in which violence regularly occurs; or, like Alicia, you might have a sibling who causes a great deal of turmoil within your home; or maybe you're preparing to audition for that prestigious music school you hope to attend after high school.

You can, however, learn how to respond to those situations with positive behaviors instead of negative ones, and to have some control over the thoughts and emotions you experience when faced with stress. Let's have a look at some healthy lifestyle options that can help you feel better prepared to deal with stressful situations, and some positive behaviors you can exhibit when faced with those situations.

TEND TO YOUR REST

Sleeping when you're feeling stressed out can be difficult, and that can result in a catch-22 situation: The more stressed you feel, the harder it can be for you to get to sleep and stay asleep, and the more your sleep is interrupted, the harder it can be to deal with stress.

Getting a good night's sleep is important, and it has been linked to overall positive health and the ability to better cope and deal with stress. Lack of sleep has been associated with some serious conditions, including lowered immune system functioning; memory impairment; increased risk for anxiety and depression; greater risk for some serious diseases, including heart disease and cancer; weight gain; and increased risk of accidents.

You might notice that it's harder to pay attention in school when you haven't gotten enough sleep the night before. You may tend to get irritable with your friends or family when you're tired; you may feel like you don't have enough energy to get through the day. You might rely on energy drinks or drinks that contain caffeine to help you get by. Many teens find themselves in a difficult situation when it comes to sleeping, through no fault of their own.

When you were younger, your body was ready for sleep at eight or nine o'clock. Those were natural times for you to go to sleep. As you entered your teen years, however, your circadian rhythm—an internal biological clock that regulates various physical processes—started to shift, and your natural time for falling asleep moved back. So, while you used to be ready to sleep at nine o'clock, you now might not be able to go to sleep until eleven or even midnight.

Schools in some places have shifted starting times so that older students begin later than younger ones, a move that makes sense in helping teens to get more sleep. Most schools, however, still require older students to start earlier than the younger ones; this means that if you have a long bus ride, you might have to get up at 5:30 or 6 A.M. to be ready on time. Such a situation is not conducive to getting the nine or nine and a half hours of sleep recommended for teenagers.

The National Sleep Foundation reported that the average 12th grader sleeps only 7.9 hours a night, more than an hour less that what's recommended. In one survey, one in four teens report having fallen asleep in class due to lack of sleep the night before.

If you're a teen who's having trouble sleeping, or you feel like you don't get enough sleep, you may have to make some lifestyle changes. Consider the following tips from the National Sleep Foundation:

> Try to sleep on the same schedule every night. This is a difficult task for teens, who tend to try to "catch up" on sleep on mornings they don't have to get up early for school or other tasks, but going to bed and getting up at roughly the same times every day can help you establish a regular sleeping schedule and improve the sleep you get.
> If you drink coffee or soda or other drinks or foods that contain caffeine, limit them to earlier in the day and avoid them for at least six to eight hours before bedtime. Remember that caffeine is present in hot and iced tea, chocolate, some prescription and nonprescription medicines, and many energy drinks. Check labels if you're not sure.
> Relax before bedtime by taking a warm bath or shower, or by listening to calming music, reading, or just sitting quietly. A lot of teens are wired to be constantly doing something and find it difficult to just relax, but sleep comes easier when you're in a relaxed state.
> Get plenty of exercise during the day, but don't exercise at night because it can make you more alert and wide awake.
> Remove distractions from your sleep area. Again, many teens pretty much live in their rooms, which makes it hard to get away from your stuff. Still, you should shut down computers, turn off the TV, and turn off your cell phone before you go to bed.
> If you can't fall asleep in the first 20 minutes or so, many experts recommend that you get up and read or engage in some other quiet activity until you feel more tired. Not being able to sleep can frustrate you and make it even more difficult to do so.

If you're experiencing serious sleep problems you should consult with a doctor, as it could indicate an underlying problem, such as sleep apnea or depression. Don't take sleep aids without first checking with a doctor.

PAY ATTENTION TO WHAT YOU EAT (AND DON'T EAT)

As with getting enough sleep, eating the proper foods can help you better handle stress. Eating well also keeps you energized, helps to keep your brain functioning properly, minimizes the chance of developing certain illnesses, and helps to regulate mood.

Unfortunately, many people slip up on healthy eating when they're under stress and fall back on "comfort foods," which tend to contain a lot of fat and carbohydrates. While eating a big bowl of ice cream or piece of pie might make you feel a little better in the short run, and is perfectly fine every now and then, making it a habit isn't a good idea. Foods that are loaded with sugar and other refined carbohydrates cause your blood sugar to rise and fall, and that can zap your energy, making it even harder to cope with stress.

The fact is that most people eat a less-healthy diet than they think they do, and teens, who are exposed to fast food, soda, and junk food on a regular basis, are likely to have diets that don't supply all the nutrients and vitamins that a body needs.

You should strive to eat foods that are low in fat and sugar, including plenty of whole grains, fruits and vegetables. Drink plenty of water and stay away from beverages containing lots of sugar or caffeine. To learn more about getting a proper balance of the foods you need, check out the U.S. Department of Agriculture's Web site, which contains My Pyramid, an interactive tool that contains nutrition information, a food planner, tracker, and other features. You can find it at www.mypyramid.gov.

Eating at regular intervals is a problem for some teens, who often are rushed and on the go. And some teens, especially girls, intentionally skip meals in an effort to consume fewer calories and control their weight. Skipping meals, however, is not a good idea for several reasons, including the fact that you tend to become overly hungry and eventually eat way more than you should in order to satisfy that hunger. It can also cause mood swings and fluctuating energy levels, making it harder to deal with stress.

Some studies have indicated that vitamin B can help to relieve stress. The B vitamins are found in whole grains, dairy products, leafy green vegetables, fish and seafood, meat and poultry, eggs, beans, and peas. You can also ask your parent or doctor about taking a B complex supplement.

LEARN TO RELAX

You might think that reading or playing video games or texting friends are good methods of relaxing—but the truth is, they're not. Those sorts of activities certainly can be enjoyable, but the true art of relaxing doesn't entail electronics or books or being in communication with someone else. It means sitting quietly in a quiet setting and just being with yourself.

Many people, especially teens, who are continuously plugged into music, information, or communications, have never learned how to relax. They simply don't know how to do it. If that applies to you, you're going to need to train yourself to relax, because relaxation is extremely important in managing stress. The ability to relax your body automatically reduces the harmful effects of stress. Real relaxation causes your breathing to slow down, which causes your blood pressure to drop and your muscles to relax. You can learn to relax your body by paying attention to how you breathe and your muscles.

Breathing. Everyone breathes, but most people don't breathe effectively or very well. Learning to control your breathing can greatly help you to learn to relax and better handle stress. When you're under stress and get tense, your breathing becomes more shallow and only the tops of your lungs fill up with air. That causes your oxygen level to fall, and your body reacts by sending stress chemicals into your bloodstream. That in turn makes you feel even more stressed, and your breathing gets increasingly shallow, causing more stress chemicals to invade your system. Learning to breathe deeply—using the muscle at the bottom of your lungs called your diaphragm—can help you to reduce this vicious circle of shallow breathing and stress. To practice deep breathing, follow these instructions:

1. Get into a comfortable position, either seated or lying down.
2. Close your eyes.
3. Put your hands on your lap, shrug your shoulders a few times, and relax your arms.
4. Slowly take deep breaths, feeling your lungs expand as you breathe.
5. Breathe rhythmically from your diaphragm, concentrating on the deepness of your breaths. Work your way up to 20 times of slowly breathing in, holding the breath for a second or two, and slowly breathing out.

Learning to breathe properly takes some practice, but it's a great tool for when you're feeling stressed. Try to take a little time each day to practice, and pay attention to how you feel. Chances are, you'll feel more focused and relaxed, and your energy level will improve. Once you've learned how to do it, you can practice deep breathing almost anywhere.

Relaxing your muscles. Progressive muscle relaxation is a technique to help relieve stress in your body. As with learning how to breathe properly, it takes some practice, but it's worth the effort. Again, you can sit or lie down, whichever is more comfortable. Just make sure you're in a quiet place where you won't be disturbed. The idea is to contract, or tighten up, a group of muscles, and then to consciously let the muscles relax. You can start at the top of your body or the bottom. If you start at the bottom, you'll tighten up your foot muscles, and then let them relax as you say the word "relax." Then you move to your ankle muscles, calf muscles, thigh muscles—all the way up your body to your face and head. Work slowly, and don't proceed to the next muscle group until you've felt the previous muscles relax. When you've tightened and relaxed all the muscle groups, take about 10 minutes to simply lie still and enjoy the feeling of being relaxed.

You might find at first that being by yourself in a very quiet setting, without even a TV or music for company, is unsettling and a little uncomfortable. Once you get used to it and learn how to relax your body, however, you'll find you're much better able to cope with stress.

MEDITATION TECHNIQUES

Learning to relax your body is a great start, but you've got to learn how to relax your mind, as well. Relaxing your mind means that you'll banish all disturbing, stressful thoughts and replace them with peaceful, soothing images. It's like transporting from a noisy, crowded hallway in school to a quiet, beautiful spot on a private beach, where you hear only the sound of the water.

A good way to accomplish that goal is to learn how to meditate, which simply means clearing your mind of clutter and move into a relaxed state of calm. Some people, such as certain monks or other religious people, spend their entire lives practicing the art of meditation. Almost anyone, however, can learn simple techniques of meditation that aid in relaxation by slowing heart rate and lowering blood pressure.

The more you practice meditating, the easier it will get and the less time you'll have to spend doing it. At first though, try to have at least 20 minutes for meditating.

Meditation goes hand-in-hand with the deep breathing and muscle relaxation described above. The first thing you should do is concentrate on your breathing, and then tense and relax your muscles. Once you've completed those exercises, sit or lie quietly and, as you breathe out, silently repeat a word or two. This repeated word or phrase, called a mantra, can simply be a sound, such as *om*, or whatever simple, calm word or words you'd like. Breathe in, and then out again, silently repeating your mantra as you do.

There are many different methods of meditating, but once you learn the trick of relaxing your mind along with your body, you'll be able to do it anywhere—even before you have to give a big presentation. Some good Web sites to learn more about meditation are listed in appendix 1 in the back of this book.

EXERCISE EVERY DAY

Most people know that exercising is good for their bodies. It's also known to improve brain function, decrease stress and tension, enhance mood, relieve anxiety and help with depression, and provide an overall sense of well-being. It's not completely understood why exercising is good for your mood, but experts say that it stimulates certain hormones that help to improve mood, gets rid of stress hormones, and increases blood flow to your brain. In other words, exercise is a really good idea. If you're already into the habit of exercising, give yourself a pat on the back and keep up the good work.

The U.S. Department of Health and Human Services recommends at least 60 minutes of moderate intensity physical activity on most and preferably all days, for people between the ages of six and 19. Moderate activity includes the following.

> ▶ Brisk walking (about three miles per hour)
> ▶ Riding a bike (at less than 10 miles an hour)
> ▶ Hiking
> ▶ Gardening or yard work
> ▶ Dancing
> ▶ Playing doubles tennis
> ▶ Jumping on a trampoline
> ▶ Rollerblading at a moderate pace or skateboarding
> ▶ Playing ping-pong
> ▶ Yoga

If you're already getting lots of moderate intensity physical activity and you want to add some more demanding forms, vigorous activity includes those listed below:

- Playing competitive sports such as soccer, basketball, or field hockey
- Running or jogging (five miles per hour)
- Riding a bike (at more than 10 miles per hour)
- Swimming laps
- Very fast walking (more than four miles per hour)
- Aerobics
- Playing singles tennis
- Karate or judo
- Circuit weight training
- Vigorous rollerblading

Sixty minutes of exercise almost every day might seem like an impossible task, but remember that it doesn't have to be done all at once. You can space out physical activity throughout the day by walking the dog at a brisk pace for 20 minutes in the morning and 20 minutes at night, jumping rope for 10 minutes when you get home from school, and pulling weeds for 10 minutes after dinner.

If those activities don't work for you, identify ones that do. Many communities offer free swimming in a school or community center, or your school may have a weight room you can use after classes or at night. Even running up and down the steps in your house for 10 minutes is a good form of exercise. If you can't put in 60 minutes a day, try for 40, or even 30. Establishing a pattern of getting some exercise every day, however you get it, can lead to big improvements in your overall health and help you to better manage stress.

TALK IT THROUGH, AND LEARN TO LISTEN

Did you ever have a problem that was really stressing you out until you poured out your heart to a friend, and all of a sudden the problem didn't seem so big anymore? Talking over a situation that's causing you stress is beneficial because it helps to clarify the situation and put it into perspective, and allows you the opportunity to receive feedback and advice.

Something that seems like a big deal in your head often doesn't seem so big once it's been verbalized. You might find out that your friend had a very similar situation and learn how she handled it. Just the fact that you have a friend with whom you can share a problem is comforting and reassuring in that you don't have to worry alone.

While your friends can seem like the most important part of your life, remember that in some cases, it's best to approach a trusted adult. If you have a problem that's very serious, such as one that involves a legal issue, a medical condition, drug or alcohol abuse, or thoughts of harming yourself, you'll need the advice and help of an adult.

Listening to others also can help with your stress levels. People who reach out and make connections with others typically enjoy better moods and greater levels of happiness than those who don't.

GET IN THE HABIT OF JOURNALING

Writing down your thoughts, concerns, joys, and fears also can help you to find clarity, figure out how to address problems, and remind you of the good things happening in your life. Recording thoughts on paper or on a computer, known as journaling, has been found to improve cognitive function, decrease stress levels, and increase immunity.

Journaling is different from keeping a calendar or diary of events. It involves writing down how you feel and think about what's happening in your life, not merely about what's going on. Even people who don't like to write have found it helpful to express their thoughts and feelings—and, remember, you don't have to worry about getting the grammar and punctuation right. Journaling is something you do for yourself, not for anyone else.

Keeping a journal of happy thoughts or what you consider to be blessings in your life also can improve your mood and ease stress. It's hard to feel stressed out when you're thinking about the great time you had on your family's vacation to the beach last summer or the special card your friend made by hand and gave you for your birthday.

BE ENCOURAGING AND SUPPORTIVE OF YOURSELF

The teen years are tough, there's no question about it. Teens can be notoriously hard on each other, and even harder on themselves. Nearly everyone has something they don't like about themselves, and sometimes it can be difficult to keep in mind the things you do appreciate about yourself. You might have a lot of negative thoughts about yourself, especially if you're getting messages from someone else that you're not good enough or you're deficient in some way.

With some practice, however, you can learn how to change those thoughts. You'll read a lot more about this in the next chapter, but briefly, you have to learn to recognize distorted thoughts when they occur. That is, when you respond to a stressful situation by automatically thinking "My life is horrible" or "Nothing ever goes right for
(continues on page 91)

Practical Ways to Reduce Your Stress Level

Get organized. Disorganization frequently leads to stressful situations when you can't find what you need or miss deadlines and assignments. Here are some tips:

1. Pick out what you're going to wear the next day the night before.

2. Put everything you want to take with you to school or work or wherever you're going in one place.

3. Get into the habit of putting things you use every day—your keys, jewelry, medications, makeup, iPod, cell phone—in the same place every time.

4. Keep a list, either on paper or electronically, of everything you have to do, and keep the list in a place where you can access it easily

5. Use a planner to keep track of all your activities.

6. Use a planner to keep track of your homework assignments and deadlines.

7. Keep your room, or your part of your room if you share, in some sort of order so that you know where things are.

8. Break down big assignments or projects into parts and do one part at a time, making sure you leave enough time to finish the entire project.

Slow down. Moving through life at a frantic speed can get to seem normal after you've done it for a while, but it is wearing and stressful. Try some of these ways of relaxing:

9. Plan a stay-at-home night and chill out with a video or a book.

10. Invite a friend or two for a "no-stress" night with facials and favorite movies.

11. If you're in a particularly busy and stressful time, reschedule a lesson or appointment and use the extra time to catch up on your work or to relax.

12. Don't overschedule yourself with social or other obligations.

13. Determine what you most enjoy and spend your time on one or two activities, rather than always jumping from one thing to another.

Here are ways to make some quiet time:

14. Take the headphones out of your ears, turn off your cell phone, get away from your computer, and just sit quietly for 15 minutes.

15. If you live in an area where you can do so, go outside and listen to sounds of nature such as birds, the wind, or crickets at night.

16. Create a small space, either indoors or out, where you can go to be alone and undisturbed, and visit it several times a week.

17. Practice deep breathing, meditation, or journaling.

18. Consider your spirituality and what it means to you.

Do something nice for someone else. Research shows that people who reach out and care about others are happier than those who don't. Try doing the following:

19. Visit an elderly relative or neighbor.

20. Take a child to the park or for a walk.

21. Tell a parent, a grandparent, or a friend that you appreciate him or her, and why.

22. Volunteer at a nursing home or assisted living facility.

23. Take your neighbor's dog for a walk or help clean up his or her yard.

24. Be aware of what other people are going through and express concern to someone who you know is experiencing a problem or difficult time.

25. Volunteer at your local library; a preschool; or your church, synagogue, or mosque.

(continues)

(continued)

Get active. Exercise is an important stress management tool, so make sure you find time to fit in some physical activity every day:

26. Keep a jump rope handy and do 100 jumps three times a day.

27. Train yourself to think of physical activity as a gift of time that you give to yourself, instead of a chore that needs to be done.

28. Engage in little bits of physical activity at a time, increasing the duration as you go.

29. Participate in an organized sport, or get a group of friends together for an informal game of football, Frisbee, or other activity.

30. Dig out the skateboard or scooter you had as a kid and give it a go.

Finally, take care of yourself, no matter what:

31. Give yourself some time before bed to relax and quiet down.

32. Try to go to bed and get up at about the same time every day.

33. Make your room as quiet and restful as you can, and turn off the TV before you go to sleep.

34. Avoid drinks that contain caffeine, especially later in the day.

35. Try to eat plenty of fruits and vegetables every day and stay away from too much fast food and processed foods, especially those that contain lots of sugar, salt, and fat.

36. Don't beat yourself up over little things you did or didn't do.

37. Don't demand perfectionism of yourself or anyone else—you won't find it!

38. Regularly take time to think about what's good in your life and practice feeling grateful.

39. Engage in an activity that you enjoy every day, even if it's only for a short time.

40. Forgive yourself when you do something wrong and forgive others for their mistakes.

(continued from page 87)
me," ask yourself if those thoughts are really true. Chances are, you'll realize a lot of those thoughts are not true at all—they are just your automatic thought responses. With some help and practice, you can change them.

Make a list of traits and qualities that you like about yourself. Maybe you've been told that you're really great with kids, and you can see that's true. Maybe you're a person to whom others come for advice, or you have the ability to make people laugh, or you bake the best brownies of anybody you know. Whatever those positive qualities are, learn to appreciate them and yourself. You're a valuable human being with a lot to offer the world.

WHAT YOU NEED TO KNOW

- ▶ If you are experiencing frequent symptoms of stress, it's time to think about making some positive lifestyle changes in order to reduce your level of stress.
- ▶ Being aware of your stressors and the thoughts, emotions and behaviors they evoke will help you to be able to identify where change is needed.
- ▶ Unhealthy responses to stress include self-injury, emotional eating, drug and alcohol abuse, overspending, withdrawal, and aggression.
- ▶ Deep-breathing and relaxation exercises can help you to feel more relaxed, calm, and energized.
- ▶ Making positive lifestyle changes, such as making sure you get enough exercise and rest and that you eat well, can go a long way toward relieving the negative effects of stress.

9

When Lifestyle Changes Aren't Enough

Claire was at the end of her rope and didn't know what to do. Her boyfriend, Mark, had just broken up with her—again. Her grades were suffering because she found it incredibly difficult to concentrate in school, and her parents were on her case about it. Her little sister was a complete brat and Claire had to share a room with her. A lot of nights she couldn't even get to sleep because her sister insisted on texting her friends until after 11 o'clock. That meant she'd be really tired again the next day, which made everything harder to deal with. What really bothered Claire, though, was the eating thing. She tried not to, but she thought about every single thing she put into her mouth and avoided eating whenever possible. When her mother noticed that Claire wasn't eating and forced her to finish a bowl of soup one night, Claire made herself throw up afterwards, making sure that nobody could hear her.

Claire had always considered herself to be pretty mature and capable of handling her life, but now she felt like everything was out of control. She'd tried exercising to help with her stress level, but she just didn't feel like she had enough energy to take a run. She had really worked on making herself eat healthy meals, but she felt like she was getting fatter and fatter and she couldn't stand how she looked. She'd tried to talk to her sister about the sleeping problem, but her sister couldn't care less about anyone but herself. She couldn't really talk to her best friends about her situation with Mark, because they didn't like him in the first place and were glad that he and Claire were no longer together.

Claire was getting increasingly distraught and feeling more and more that her life was out of control and she'd never be happy again. Her stress level was at an all-time high, her life felt like it was falling apart, and she was at a loss for how to deal with it all.

KNOWING WHEN IT'S TIME TO ASK FOR HELP

Sometimes it's very difficult, or even impossible, to handle a situation on your own, and you'll need to ask someone to help you. It's not always easy to do that, because our society teaches us that it's important to be strong and self reliant. Even though the perception has changed somewhat, there's still a level of admiration for people who are perceived to be tough and powerful and in control.

As you get older, however, you'll begin to understand that very, very few people make it through life without any problems, and nearly everyone reaches points in their lives when it's wise to reach out to a trusted friend, family member, or professional for some help. Our everyday lives continue to become more and more stressful, and increasing numbers of people, like Claire, are exhibiting the results of all that stress. So, how do you know when you've moved past the stage where you can handle a stressful situation on your own, and it's now time to ask someone for some help?

The lifestyle changes you made didn't improve the situation. You stopped drinking anything with caffeine in it and you made it a point to run for two miles every day. You've tried hard to get on a good nighttime schedule to assure that you'd get enough sleep, and that situation has improved. All of those changes that you worked so hard to implement, though, haven't made you feel any better. If anything, you're feeling more stressed out, because the exercise takes time away from your homework or your down time, and you end up feeling frustrated and overwhelmed.

You were unable to implement the lifestyle changes that you recognize as desirable. You really wanted to start eating better, because you thought that would give you more energy and then you'd be able to get some exercise every day, and maybe you'd feel better. However, the healthy eating didn't seem to work out. You just couldn't force yourself to eat the sandwich you'd bring for lunch because you didn't feel in the least bit hungry. You'd just play with your food at dinner, and you never were a breakfast eater, so that wasn't an issue. When you did get hungry, you'd just grab a soda or an energy drink and maybe a granola bar or an apple or something. You're always feeling tired, so it's impossible to get any exercise. You feel like a real loser because you couldn't make the changes you wanted to, but that's just the way it's going right now.

The cause of your stress never lets up. No matter what kind of grades you get, your dad always yells at you and tells you they aren't good enough. Even when you had all As and just one B, he was upset about the B and angry that you were only taking two honors courses when some other kids were taking three. When he's not complaining about your grades he finds something else to yell at you for—a messy room, forgetting to empty the dishwasher, not taking the dog out often enough. He always finds something to upset him, and it seems like it's always you he picks on.

The cause of your stress has subsided, but you still feel overwhelmed and anxious. You thought you'd feel so much better when your uncle, who'd been staying at your house for a couple of months, moved out. Not that you don't love your uncle, but he really made you nervous when he was around. He always stood too close to you and he touched you a lot in ways that seemed creepy and weird. He paid too much attention to you and would come into your room while you were doing your homework and stand behind you, sometimes rubbing your shoulders. You tried to talk to your mom about it, but she said you were just being silly and imagining things, even though you felt really scared and anxious. He finally moved out a couple of weeks ago, but you find that you're still feeling on edge and uneasy. You've been having some bad dreams and finding it hard to get a good night's sleep, and your grades have been slipping because you feel so distracted and fretful.

If any of those situations apply to you—if you've made lifestyle changes that haven't helped, have tried but found you're unable to make desirable lifestyle changes, are experiencing unrelenting stress, or have stress that's subsided but you still feel anxious and uneasy—you should consider asking for some help. Someone trained in stress management can help you in a number of ways, by teaching you several tactics and strategies:

> ‣ How to better cope with common stressors
> ‣ New skills and resources that will help you deal with situations that need to change

➤ How to implement the skills and resources that will help bring about change

➤ How to better deal with situations that won't change

There is no shame in asking for help, and you and those around you will benefit once you do.

KNOWING WHO TO ASK FOR HELP

If you're lucky, you have what's called a support system. Simply stated, your support system is the people in your life with whom you can talk about your problems and concerns. Some people have small support systems made up of only one or two people, while others have extended support systems.

Lisa, for instance, is an only child, a 15-year-old girl who lives with her mom. Her mom and dad are divorced and she hardly ever sees her father, who remarried and moved to a different state when Lisa was just three years old. Her grandparents have either died or live far away, and she has only two cousins, both of whom live in another part of the country. Lisa's pretty shy and it's never been easy for her to make friends, especially because she and her mom tend to move around a lot, depending on her mom's boyfriend and job situations.

When Lisa has a big problem, the only person she feels comfortable approaching is her mom, who often is too busy or distracted to pay much attention to her. The situation is even more complicated for Lisa recently, because her latest problem—and it's a big one—is that her mom's new boyfriend made a serious pass at her and has been making inappropriate remarks. Lisa is thinking about going to see a guidance counselor at school, but she feels like she'd be intruding and the counselor might get angry. Lisa, unfortunately, and for a number of reasons, has a very limited support system.

David, on the other hand, has a large support system. He's not one of the "popular crowd," but the 16-year-old has a lot of friends whom he trusts and with whom he's comfortable. He's in the marching and concert bands at school, and he and other band members hang out together all year long. David is also involved with the chess club, sings in his church's choir and is active in the youth group, so he's usually pretty busy and involved with others.

His mom and dad live together and get along pretty well, and, although David doesn't agree with everything they do, he's got to admit that they take good care of him and his brother and sister. It's easier sometimes to talk to a friend about a problem, but David knows that his parents will help him when he needs it. He's also friendly with a couple of adults at his church, and they've told him more than once to let them know if he ever needs anything. He sees his cousins pretty often because they live nearby and the families get together for picnics or trips sometimes. And David is really close to his granddad, who lives just one town over.

When David got into a situation—a friend of his stole a pair of sunglasses from a store at the mall when David was with him and was caught on film and apprehended by store security—David was incredibly upset because he thought he'd be in big trouble too, even though he didn't even know his friend had taken the glasses. David agonized over whether or not to "fess up" to his parents about what had happened, and the situation became very stressful for him. Fortunately, he was able to talk to his grandfather about it, who accompanied his grandson when David explained the situation to his parents, as his grandfather had encouraged him to do.

It's easy to see the differences between Lisa's and David's situations concerning support systems. Most people's support systems fall somewhere in between those examples, and, many people rely heavily on their friends and relatives when problems occur. Who might you turn to when you have a problem that you feel you can't resolve on your own?

A *parent or other relative*. Talking to your parent, or perhaps a grandparent or aunt or uncle, is a great approach for addressing a problem that you consider serious. Sometimes, however, for whatever reasons, teens are uncomfortable discussing certain topics with parents and may seek out someone else.

A *friend or several friends*. Friends who will listen to your concerns and understand you are wonderful resources, and there's nothing wrong with sharing your problems with them. But friends often don't have the answers to serious problems or the resources to help you change a troublesome situation. So remember that while it might be good for you to share your problem and get it out into the open, there are times when your friends may simply not be equipped to help you.

A *trusted teacher, youth group leader, or other adult*. A trusted adult is a great idea for someone who will listen to you and assist you in getting additional help, if necessary. Some problems, however, require the expertise of a mental health professional who has been trained in diagnosing and treating conditions relating to stress and anxiety.

A pediatrician who you know. Many teens have been seeing the same pediatrician for a long time and have gotten to know that person. You might ask your parent to make an appointment with your pediatrician, or your parent might suggest that you see him or her. Either way, it's a good idea, because a pediatrician can rule out a physical problem that could be presenting symptoms that mimic those caused by stress. A thyroid problem, for instance, could cause you to feel tired and depressed, much like significant amounts of stress can.

FINDING A MENTAL HEALTH PROFESSIONAL

Some stress-related conditions will require the expertise of a mental health professional who can assess the situation and provide treatment. Mental health professionals are trained to treat mental, emotional, and behavioral disorders. If you have tried talking to your friends or parents or other trusted adults and have not gotten the relief you'd hoped for, you should consider contacting a mental health professional.

Mental health is by no means a new subject or new area of study, but some people still find it to be mysterious and even threatening, which makes them reluctant to seek help for mental health issues. Some people consider asking for help to be a sign of weakness, but that couldn't be further from the truth. Not being afraid to ask for some help is a smart and strong decision, and it indicates that you're stepping up to the plate to take charge of a situation. So, congratulations!

If you've been to a pediatrician to rule out any sort of physical problem or have talked to a school counselor or a parent, one of them may have already recommended that you seek professional help and that he or she can assist you in doing so. It's possible that your mom talked to Andrea's mom, who recommended a psychologist who helped Andrea through a rough spot a few months back, and your mom has decided to call that professional. If you're looking for a mental health expert on your own, however, or you're working to help your parent identify someone, you may need a little direction before making a decision about whom to call. There are various types of mental health professionals, some of which will have more experience treating stress-related problems than others.

Generally, patients suffering from stress-related problems are most successful when they are treated with cognitive-behavioral therapy, a form of psychotherapy in which therapists help their clients to better manage problems by helping them to change the way they think,

Working Within the Confines of Your Insurance Plan

While it's important to know what sort of mental health treatment is available in your area, it well may be that your insurer ultimately will have a large say in who you will see. It's common for an insurer, including Medicaid, to offer a list of approved providers from which you'll need to choose your provider. If that's the case, get as familiar as you can with the providers on the list in order to help you make an informed decision about whom to call.

behave, and respond to various situations. Cognitive therapy has been proven to be useful in treating an array of disorders, including those associated with stress. Therapists who use this model are have had special training and have done extensive educational and clinical work.

To locate a thoroughly trained cognitive therapist in your area, you can check out the Academy of Cognitive Therapy Web site at http://www.academyofct.org, which includes a state-by-state directory. Another site to try is the Association for Behavioral and Cognitive Therapies, at http://www.aabt.org.

You should be aware that there are different types of specialists who work with patients suffering from stress-related problems. You might be referred to a psychiatrist, psychologist, licensed professional counselor, or a clinical social worker. All of these professionals are licensed and certified to provide treatment. However, others, such as pastoral counselors and psychotherapists, may or may not be licensed and certified. That doesn't mean that a pastoral counselor or a psychotherapist (which is a general name for just about anyone who provides counseling) can't provide valuable treatment, it's just that those professions aren't as closely regulated as those that require licensing.

Psychiatrist. A psychiatrist must have completed four years of medical school and at least three years of residency training in medicine, neurology, and general psychiatry. Psychiatrists are medical doctors who specialize in diagnosing and treating mental conditions, and are qualified to prescribe medicines. Psychiatrists must be certified by the board of psychiatry and neurology, and pass licensing tests in the states in which they will practice. With extra training, a psychiatrist can become board-certified in child and adolescent psychiatry. All psychiatrists must pass written and oral exams, and must be recertified every 10 years.

Psychologist. There are several varieties of psychologists, including clinical psychologists, developmental psychologists, school psychologists, and counseling psychologists. The most common type of psychologist in a treatment setting is a clinical psychologist—someone who has earned a doctoral degree and are qualified to diagnose and treat mental, emotional, and behavioral disorders. Psychologists in most states are not licensed to prescribe medicines, so they often work closely with psychiatrists who can provide prescriptions when necessary. Clinical psychologists help patients with both short- and long-term problems, and some specialize in certain types of problems, such as anxiety or depression, while others specialize in treating certain populations, such as adolescents or the elderly.

A developmental psychologist specializes in what is going on with a person during a specific time of life, such as childhood or adolescence, and can measure behaviors and development as they compare to others in the same period of life. A school psychologist works with students, parents, and school personnel to address behavioral issues and other difficulties encountered in the school setting. School psychologists often hold master's degrees instead of doctoral degrees. A counseling psychologist works with clients in matters of day-to-day life, helping them to find strategies to cope with problems and draw on their strengths to achieve goals.

Psychologists work in various settings, including hospitals, clinics, schools, and private practices. Because there are various types of psychologists, it's important to find one who has good training and experience in the areas in which you'll be looking for help. If you're seeking treatment for a stress-related problem, you probably should identify a psychologist with clinical experience to help you. Look for someone who is certified and licensed in the state in which he or she is practicing.

Licensed professional counselor. A licensed professional counselor must hold at least a master's degree in counseling or a related field, successfully complete supervised clinical training, and be certified by the state in which he or she will practice. These counselors employ various strategies to address wellness, personal growth, and other areas of concern.

Social worker. You might think of a social worker as someone who works with poor people or families in which parents have trouble caring for their children, but some social workers—called clinical social workers—are licensed or certified to work with clients in a clinical setting to prevent, diagnose, and treat mental, behavioral, and emotional disorders. Requirements vary from state to state, but all clinical social workers must have a master's or doctoral degree in social work, with an emphasis on clinical experience; have completed an internship; and have completed at least two years of supervised clinical social work.

Pastoral counselor. If you look in the counseling section of your phone book, you'll probably notice the title "pastoral counselor." A pastoral counselor has completed both theological and psychological training, and addresses problems in terms of religion and spirituality. Some pastoral counselors are licensed, but most states do not provide licensing. An advantage of pastoral counselors is that their fees generally are lower than those of some other types of mental health professionals. However, most insurance plans won't cover pastoral counseling unless the counselor is licensed.

Psychotherapist. The term *psychotherapist* can refer to almost anyone, licensed or otherwise, who provides counseling services. Counselors range from psychiatrists to ministers, as well as social workers, psychologists, marriage counselor, addictions counselors, and psychiatric nurses. While there is a room for all types of counselors, when you're working to address a problem that's become serious to you and is affecting your life, it's important to know who you're working with and be sure the person is qualified and credentialed.

Regardless of the type of professional you end up going to, it's extremely important that you find out the person's level of experience in treating stress-related disorders and in using cognitive therapy. Don't be afraid to ask questions and look for information online. Ask questions about the average length of treatment for a patient with a stress-related disorder and how many people suffering from your particular problem the person has treated. Sources such as Angie's list, which contain actual feedback about doctors from patients and others, are controversial, and you need to use those sorts of sites cautiously. However, you usually can look online to learn about a professional's educational credentials, clinical training, years of experience, licensing status, and so forth.

TAKING CARE OF BUSINESS BEFORE TREATMENT BEGINS

Once you've identified a mental health professional and made an appointment, it seems reasonable to expect that you'll show up at the right time and begin treatment for your stress-related problem. If you've been to a new doctor any time recently, you might know that probably won't be the scenario you'll experience.

Some part of your first visit to the professional who will be treating you is likely to be spent filling out forms. Unless you've made the appointment on your own and do not have the support of a family member, you'll need to have a parent or guardian with you to sign some of the forms.

You'll probably be asked to read information regarding the practice's privacy policy and fill out forms such as a statement of financial responsibility (normally a parent completes that one), a personal history questionnaire, an authorization for release of protected health information, and possibly other forms. You'll be asked to answer a

---

Consenting to Mental Health Treatment

What happens is you decide that you need mental health treatment, but your parent or guardian doesn't consent? It varies from state to state, but, in Pennsylvania, for example, a teen who is 14 or older can declare that he needs treatment, and that overrides the decision of the parent or guardian. So, in that state, a teen can sign his own consent-to-treatment form and receive treatment, provided that he's able to pay and be accountable for getting to treatment and so forth. On the other hand, parents can require a teen to be placed in the care of a mental health professional, even if the teen doesn't want to go. It's a little confusing, and mental health treatment usually works better if the parents and teen are in agreement that it's necessary and useful. If there are any issues between you and your parent regarding the need for treatment, be open and candid, and try to work out some sort of agreement before care begins.

lot of questions that are very personal, but it's extremely important to be honest—that way, the professional who will be treating you can get an accurate assessment of what's going on and learn what issues need to be addressed.

Some teens find it difficult to be completely truthful when they fill out personal history forms and questionnaires, which normally include questions concerning smoking, drug and alcohol use, and may contain questions about sexual history and other issues about which teens may be reluctant to share information. If you are asked to answer such questions, remember that an experienced health-care professional will have treated a great many patients, and it's extremely unlikely that he or she will be disturbed or shocked by anything you write on the form. As a patient, it's your responsibility to be honest in order to best facilitate treatment.

Under normal circumstances, before your treatment starts, you, your parents or guardian, and the therapist will have a conversation regarding what type of information will be shared with your parents, and what will remain confidential between you and the therapist. You might agree that parents will sit in on any sessions regarding medical problems, such as stress-related headaches, but will not be present for sessions during which you discuss situations in school that are making you feel stressed and causing problems. Joint sessions may be scheduled to deal with problems between your parents and you or other family members.

These situations vary from patient to patient and family to family, and it sometimes can be challenging to reach an agreement that suits all involved parties, but it's important that an understanding is in place before therapy begins. You should realize that while conversations between a health-care professional and a patient are generally confidential, a doctor or other mental health-care provider is obligated by law to report it if someone is threatening to harm himself or others. On the flip side, the same law may prevent a doctor from informing parents of issues such as repeated drug use. Much of what a doctor shares with parents will be determined by the conversation among the three parties prior to the start of treatment, so you can see that it's important that the conversation takes place and all the parties involved share the same expectations.

WHAT TO EXPECT DURING TREATMENT

Once all the forms are filled out and everyone is in agreement regarding how and when information will be shared, you'll have your first session with the doctor or therapist. Note that the description of treatment that follows pertains to cognitive-behavioral therapy, which was described earlier in the chapter. Other types of therapies will vary from what you'll be reading about here, but, if you choose cognitive therapy, this will give you a good idea of what you can expect.

During your first session, your doctor or therapist will ask you a lot of questions in order to get to know you and to find out what's going on in your life that is resulting in stress. It's important for the therapist to understand the full context in which stress is occurring, which means he will ask you questions regarding a wide variety of issues. If you say that you're stressed out about your grades, for instance, the therapist might ask you questions regarding the following:

> Physical problems or conditions
> Learning disabilities
> Peer relationships and pressures
> Boyfriend or girlfriend issues
> Parental relationships
> Homework habits
> Psychological history
> Social relationships
> Other problems in school, such as bullying
> Sleeping habits
> Pressure placed on you by yourself and others

You might think that some of the questions are stupid, or that the therapist is incredibly nosy, but you should trust that he knows what he's doing and the information he's seeking is necessary in order to identify the real causes of stress and be able to help you make changes.

The therapist will look at how stress is occurring on several levels, and will ask you questions to learn how it is affecting you. For instance, he or she might ask, do you experience headaches or knots in your stomach? Do you tend to freeze up when confronted with a stressful situation? Does your mind go blank? Do you break out in a sweat, or feel nauseous, or scared, or panicky? Understanding the ways in which stress is causing you pain is necessary in order for the therapist to help you get past the pain.

After the doctor or therapist has gathered a broad range of information, he'll begin asking you some very pointed and specific questions. And he'll ask you to tell him about a recent experience during which you were very stressed. The conversation might sound something like this:

Doctor Miller: So, give me an example of an experience you had recently that caused you to feel really stressed out.

Rachel: We had a chemistry test last week and I knew I wasn't going to do well on it.

Dr. Miller: Well, tell me what you were thinking when the teacher handed out the test.

Rachel: I was thinking that I was going to flunk it.

Dr. Miller: How were you feeling when she handed out the test?

Rachel: I was feeling really scared.

Dr. Miller: How did you react when the test was handed out?

Rachel: My mind went blank and I couldn't concentrate.

Dr. Miller: Well, if you would flunk the test, what does that mean about you?

Rachel: It means that I'm stupid and I can't do anything right.

Dr. Miller: Okay, I see.

At this point, Rachel has revealed both her automatic thought and her core belief, both of which are very significant in cognitive-behavioral therapy. Rachel's automatic thought was that she was going to flunk the test, and that triggered the emotion of feeling scared, and the behavior of blanking out and not being able to concentrate. The thought of flunking the test led her back to her core belief of being stupid and unable to do anything right.

Core beliefs are established in different ways, and they usually apply to many areas of a person's life. Certain personality traits may make a person vulnerable to possessing a core belief that he or she is stupid and unable to do anything right, but it's more likely that the belief is a result of what he or she has heard and experienced.

In Rachel's case, for instance, her parents pushed her very hard and expressed serious disappointment when her grades were not at the top of her class. They did this because they want Rachel to get into a great college, graduate with honors, get a terrific job, and be highly successful. Rachel, however, perceives that they're pushing her because they believe she's incapable of getting good grades on her own, or doing anything else on her own, for that matter. She's come to the conclusion that she's stupid and can't do anything right, and this belief affects many areas of her life and the relationships she has with others.

The job of the therapist, in a case like Rachel's, is to help her to recognize her automatic thought and her core belief, to evaluate her beliefs and to develop alternative beliefs. Rachel and Dr. Miller would first work on replacing her automatic thought with another one.

> Dr. Miller: So, you were thinking that you were going to flunk the test.
>
> Rachel: That's right. I was sure that I would.
>
> Dr. Miller: How many tests this year have you already flunked?
>
> Rachel: Well, I haven't flunked any tests.
>
> Dr. Miller: Oh. What grades do you normally get on tests?
>
> Rachel: I almost always get As or Bs.

While evaluating her belief, Rachel realizes that her automatic thought is not consistent with her personal experiences. At this point she can work to change it. Her new thought might be something like this: "I know that I get nervous when I have to take a test, but there's no reason to think I'm going to flunk it, because I always do quite well. I know that I studied hard for this test. I'll do my best and it will probably work out the same as it has in the past."

Of course, this thought won't come automatically for a while, and Rachel will be tempted to fall back on her old automatic thought that she would flunk the test. By being aware of the situation, however, she can redirect her thoughts toward the new statement. Replacing the old automatic thought with a new one will lead to changed emotions and behaviors. Instead of feeling really scared when the test is handed out, Rachel will feel just a little nervous. And, instead of blanking out and not being able to concentrate, she'll be aware of her heart beating a little faster than normal, but she won't lose her ability to stay focused on the test. Changing her automatic thought to one based on her actual experiences will help Rachel to deal with the stress associated with test taking and build up her confidence.

Addressing and changing the automatic thought and the reactions that result from it is the first part of the cognitive therapy process. Addressing and changing the core belief is a little more difficult.

TREATING THE CORE BELIEF

Rachel's core belief, which has resulted from a variety of factors, is that she is stupid and unable to do anything right. Her life circumstances, however, do not support that belief. She doesn't flunk tests;

in fact, she does very well in school. She doesn't wreck the car every time she drives; in fact, she passed her driving test on the first try and has never had a problem with the car. She doesn't get to the grocery store and not know why she's there; in fact, her mother often sends her out on errands. Rachel has plenty of friends who care about her, and she's active in her church's youth group. Generally, she's a well-rounded individual who navigates life perfectly fine.

The work of Rachel and Dr. Miller is to identify situations that trigger Rachel's core belief so she's aware of when that belief is likely to negatively affect her, and to replace the core belief with a different one.

Rachel might realize that her core belief of being stupid kicks in when she's confronted with taking a test, talking with her father about current events, eating dinner with her family—even, sometimes, when she's playing board games with friends. Upon closer examination, however, she also begins to realize that there is no evidence to support her core belief, and quite a bit of evidence that proves it wrong.

After that realization, Dr. Miller will help Rachel to come up with an alternate core belief, such as this: "This situation [such as taking a test or talking with her father] often triggers my core belief that I'm stupid, but a review of evidence from my life does not support my belief. The evidence suggests that I am competent at a lot of things, and if I keep that in mind, I will probably do pretty well at most of what I attempt."

Changing a core belief doesn't happen in one therapy session, or overnight, or in a week. It can take months of working and talking to yourself and substituting the new core belief for the old. Patients who are willing to do that work, however, very often can change the way they view their lives and themselves, and learn to more easily cope with stressful situations. If you're working with a therapist, be prepared to continue the work on your own between sessions. Typically, you'd see the therapist once a week at first. It's very easy to forget from one session to the next what you'd covered, and a waste of time to have to review what's already been done. Ask your doctor for homework between sessions, and be prepared to devote a fair amount of time to your treatment—you'll find that it's well worth the effort.

Treatment with a cognitive-behavior therapist can last from a few months for simple issues to several years for more serious ones. Many people schedule appointments on and off after they've stopped therapy on a regular basis, and that can be very helpful when you're anticipating a stressful situation. Therapy doesn't work in the same manner for every patient, and it's important to take your time in determining what works best for you.

MEDICINES USED TO TREAT STRESS-RELATED PROBLEMS

Many doctors recommend a combination of therapy and medication for significant stress-related problems, such as depression or anxiety. In fact, a recent study by the National Institute of Mental Health, a division of the governmental agency the National Institutes of Health, revealed that a combination of therapy and medication was more effective than either therapy or medication alone when treating teens suffering from moderate to severe depression.

If a doctor or psychiatrist prescribes medicine for you, he or she probably will suggest that you work with a psychologist or other type of counselor to determine the best course of action for your treatment. Conversely, if you begin treatment with a psychologist or other type of therapist who does not prescribe medicine, the therapist might request that a doctor or psychiatrist review the potential benefits of medicine with you.

If your doctor or therapist recommends that you take medication, it's important to find out everything you can about the medicine prescribed and follow your doctor's directions as to how to take it. Make sure the prescribing doctor knows about any other medications—including vitamins and herbal supplements—you might be taking. If you take asthma medicine, for instance, it's important to make that known. Ask how often you should take the medicine, if you need to take it with food or milk, if it is likely to cause any side effects, what happens if you feel better and think you no longer need the medicine, and how long you might expect to take it.

If paying for medicine is a problem for you or your family, there are some options for getting it at a reduced cost or for free. More information about that is available in chapter 11, "Paying for Care."

A variety of medicines are used in treating teens who suffer from stress-related disorders such as depression and anxiety. You'll notice that some of the same meds are used to treat both of those conditions. Drugs commonly used to treat anxiety include the following:

- Selective serotonin reuptake inhibitors (SSRIs)
- Tricyclic antidepressants
- Benzodiazepines

Drugs commonly used to treat depression include the following:

- Selective serotonin reuptake inhibitors (SSRIs)
- Tricyclic antidepressants

➤ Serotonin norepinephrine reuptake inhibitors (SNRIs)
➤ Monoamine oxidase inhibitors (MAOIs)

It's important to know that you might have to try more than one course of treatment until you find a medicine that is effective for you. Sometimes a doctor will prescribe of combination of meds, and often, dosages need to be adjusted.

If you are prescribed medicine and, as is hoped, start feeling much better, don't stop taking your meds without consulting your doctor. And, because some studies have suggested a link between certain drugs used to treat depression and teen suicide, it's important to tell someone right away if you begin feeling hopeless, overwhelmed, or have thoughts of harming yourself.

WHAT YOU NEED TO KNOW

➤ It can be extremely difficult, or impossible, to handle an ongoing, highly stressful situation on your own. If you feel that you're unable to do so, the smartest thing to do is to ask for help.

➤ It may be time to ask for help for your stress-related problem if you've tried lifestyle changes and they didn't work, if you were unable to implement the lifestyle changes you wanted to, if the cause of your stress is ongoing and never stops, or if the cause of your stress has stopped but you still feel anxious and overwhelmed.

➤ If you feel like you need to talk to someone about the circumstances that are causing you great stress, look first to your support system, which may include parents, grandparents, trusted neighbors or other relatives, friends, a school nurse, youth group leader, pediatrician, and so forth.

➤ If you don't get the relief you're looking for from members of your support system, consider contacting a mental health professional, who is specially trained to treat mental, emotional, and behavioral disorders, and will be able to assess your situation and provide treatment.

➤ Cognitive-behavioral therapy, either by itself or combined with medication, has been proven to be an effective method of treating stress-related problems in teenagers.

➤ Mental health professionals include psychiatrists, psychologists, clinical social workers, licensed professional counselors, pastoral counselors, and psychotherapists.

- ➤ Once you've located a mental health professional, you can usually look online to learn about his or her educational credentials, clinical training, years of experience, licensing status, and so forth.
- ➤ You'll be asked to fill out a lot of forms and provide a lot of information before actual therapy begins. It's important to cooperate and provide accurate, complete information.
- ➤ It may seem like your doctor or therapist is incredibly nosy, but he or she needs to obtain a wide variety of information in order to be able to assess your situation and help you overcome your stress-related problems.
- ➤ A cognitive-behavioral therapist will work with patients to help them evaluate destructive automatic thoughts and to change their core beliefs.
- ➤ Various medications are available to treat stress-related problems in teens. If you're prescribed medicine, be proactive and learn all you can about it, how it works, possible side effects, and so forth.

10

Helping Others Deal with Stress

Chris had always been a friendly, well-liked kid. He was a member of the student council, swam backstroke on the swim team, and sang in the school chorus. He had a younger sister with whom he seemed to get along pretty well, and he and his mom and sister went to church most Sundays. When Chris was in the first half of 11th grade, however, his friends noticed that his personality seemed to change. He became withdrawn, and often seemed angry. He didn't laugh much anymore, and he was hanging out with a different group of kids than he used to.

His friends were concerned and tried to talk to Chris, but he just kept on saying that everything was fine; he just felt like being with different people sometimes. His friends noticed that Chris was acting different in school now, talking back to teachers and getting into trouble. His grades were in trouble, too, and it seemed like he just didn't care.

One Friday night after a school football game, two of Chris's friends saw his car in a parking lot across from the stadium and went over to say hello. When they got there they discovered that Chris was in the car with two kids they didn't know very well, smoking marijuana and drinking beer.

Now Chris's friends were really concerned, and kind of angry, as well. They thought Chris was acting like a jerk for no reason and turning his back on those who'd been his friends since fifth or sixth grade. Chris didn't return any of their texts that weekend and didn't show up on Facebook, either. He seemed to be pulling further and further away from them. Upset and concerned, Chris's friends talked over the situation and made a decision to confront him about what was happening.

Pulling Chris aside after school one day, they convinced him to come to Jack's house to hang out for a little while. Once there, they expressed their concerns and told him they were upset with how Chris had been acting. Chris didn't want to talk at first, and he even got a little mad, but finally he told them that his dad was in serious trouble for stealing money from his employer, and probably was going to be arrested soon. His dad had been drinking a whole lot, and his mom and dad fought all the time. Chris also suspected that his dad had been having an affair, and was afraid his parents would end up getting divorced. He was worried about his mom and sister, and really, really angry at his dad.

Once Chris had told his friends what had been going on, they understood that he'd been under tremendous stress and had been acting out in an effort to relieve that stress. They convinced him to talk to the swim coach about what was going on, and the coach was understanding and helpful.

In the end, it turned out that Chris's dad wasn't arrested, but ended up going into rehab to address his drinking and other problems. It was a rough time and took a lot of work on everyone's part, but eventually, with the help of a good counselor, the family was able to work out some of its problems and begin to move forward.

Chris probably never expressed it to his friends, but he would always be thankful that they didn't give up on him and cared enough to insist that he tell them what was happening.

If you have a friend or loved one who you suspect is very stressed out, you can stand by that person and offer your help. Stress-related problems easily can lead to depression, anxiety, and other disorders, so it's important to address them early. What, then, can you do?

FIND YOUR FRIEND SOME HELP

If you have a friend or relative who you believe is experiencing significant stress-related problems, the most important thing you can do is steer that person toward some help. You might suggest, as Chris's friends did, that he or she talk to a teacher, coach, or guidance counselor. Offer to go with her. If she's hesitant, you could say something like, "Hey, it's not a big deal. Let's just go and hear what the guidance counselor has to say."

Because you're reading this book, it's a good bet that you've experienced some periods of considerable stress in your own life. Perhaps you've already benefited from talking to someone about what was occurring and you could say to your friend: "I remember when I was so stressed out after Drew broke up with me. I really felt better when I talked to Mrs. Smith about it." Knowing that you've experienced similar feelings and were able to cope better after asking for help may be reassuring to your friend.

If you suspect that your friend is suffering from depression, a condition often related to stress, it's very important that you suggest that

Knowing When It's Time to Talk to an Adult

Nobody wants to be a snitch or rat out a friend. Sometimes, though, the best thing you can do for someone you care about is to tell a trusted adult what's going on. If you have a friend who you believe is depressed, that's grounds for going to an adult. Same for if your friend is engaging in risky behaviors, such as using drugs and/or alcohol, driving after using drugs and/or alcohol, engaging in unsafe sex, possessing a weapon, participating in criminal activity, or associating with people who are participating in criminal activity.

If you suspect your friend might be considering suicide, you need to tell an adult immediately. In addition, encourage him or her to call the National Suicide Prevention Lifeline, which has a toll-free 24-hour hotline that is staffed by trained counselors. The number is 1-800-273-TALK. If your friend is in immediate danger of harming himself or herself, call 911.

No matter how angry or upset your friend might get, alerting an adult to the situation and starting the process of getting your friend some help is worth it. He or she will eventually realize that you went to the adult because you cared and wanted him or her to feel better, and that you may have saved his or her life.

she see a doctor in order to get an appropriate diagnosis and treatment. If left untreated, depression can lead to suicidal thoughts and even suicidal acts. Suicide is the third-leading cause of death among young people between the ages of 15 and 24, and the sixth-leading cause of those between five and 14, according to the American Academy of Child & Adolescent Psychiatry.

Not everyone who is depressed experiences the same symptoms, which are listed in chapter 7, but if your friend seems very sad, hopeless, restless or irritable, tired, or withdrawn; or is experiencing sleeping problems, eating too much or too little; or having physical symptoms like headaches, ongoing aches and pains, cramps, and digestive problems that don't go away, you're right to be concerned.

While it's difficult sometimes to approach someone you know and suggest that he or she might need to get some help, it's the best thing you can do for a friend suffering from stress-related problems or depression. Hopefully, your friend will agree, either now, or in the future.

What happens, though, if your friend becomes upset or angry at your suggestion? Maybe he or she doesn't want to talk about it, or he or she is embarrassed. If you are genuinely concerned about a friend and he or she refuses to ask someone for help, it's important that you talk to an adult you trust about the situation. Hopefully, that adult will contact your friend's family or another adult who can intervene and take charge of the situation.

PROVIDE EMOTIONAL SUPPORT

As a teenager who has experienced your own share of stress, you're in a good position to be understanding and empathetic toward your friend. Chances are you can remember what it's like to feel your heart beating too fast, or your stomach clenching, or being unable to sleep, or feeling like you want to pig out on junk food all the time because it makes you feel a little bit better. Understanding those feelings lets you be empathetic and offer support to others experiencing those same feelings. You can't, of course, totally understand another person's thoughts and feelings, but when you talk to them you can project understanding and empathy.

The definition of *empathy* is "the action of understanding, being aware of, being sensitive to, and vicariously experiencing the feelings, thoughts, and experience of another of either the past or present without having the feelings, thoughts, and experience fully communicated in an objectively explicit manner."

All that means is that a person who is empathetic can understand what someone else is experiencing and feeling without the other person verbalizing it, often because the empathetic person has been through a similar or same situation.

If you know someone who is struggling with problems related to stress, you can help by offering emotional support. Emotional support can come in the form of a hug, a touch on the arm, an offer to talk, or sometimes just a smile. Letting your friend know that you understand he or she is struggling is a form of support. So is sharing your feelings and letting him or her know you're open to talking and listening. Sharing your experiences and how you coped with your own problems are good means of emotional support, but don't spend so much time talking about yourself that you neglect to really listen to him or her; sometimes, even when we're listening to someone else, we're really thinking about what we'd like to say and just waiting for a chance to jump in.

Experts advise that, in order to be an effective listener, you should keep the following tips in mind:

- Once the other person begins talking, just listen. Don't interrupt or interject information or your thoughts—just listen. Maintain eye contact with the person speaking and actively indicate that you're listening by nodding or other gestures.
- When your friend is done talking, summarize back to her what she told you, focusing on how you think she must feel. You could say something like: "Wow. You've really got a lot going on with college boards coming up this weekend, your dad being in the hospital, and you mom losing her job. It sounds like you're having a hard time handling all that."
- Ask your friend to clarify how she's feeling. This will give you a better idea of her state of mind and may help her to feel better by expressing her feelings.
- Don't be tempted to shift the focus onto yourself right away, even if you've been in a similar situation. Wait until she's had her say, and then you can share your experience and how you handled it.
- Don't jump in with advice until your friend has had her say. Often, just explaining a problem or situation out loud provides enough clarity that the person experiencing it can figure out a solution on her own. Once she's had time to say everything she wants to, you and she can put your heads

together to come up with some suggestions for how she might solve the problem.

BE A DEPENDABLE PRESENCE

Someone who is experiencing problems related to stress, like Chris was, might not be pleasant or fun to be with. Instead of looking forward to being with your friend, you might actually start to dread seeing him or her. You might be tempted to avoid your friend because it's easier to just not deal with his or her attitude, or sadness, or worries.

Avoiding your friend, however, could make him or her feel abandoned or rejected, or think you no longer care about him or her. When someone is under a great deal of stress, the last thing he or she needs is to feel is abandoned. Even if your friend's behavior is difficult and annoying, try to remember that now is the time she needs you the most. If Chris's friends hadn't stuck by him and maintained a dependable presence during his time of difficulty, who knows what further trouble he might have gotten into, or if his stress would have led to serious depression or other problems?

A person who is going through a tough time because of stress needs to be reassured of friendship. You can do this by continuing to call or text your friend and asking him or her to do things together. If he or she doesn't feel like going out to the mall or the movies because he or she doesn't want to be around a lot of people or is afraid others won't understand what's going on, offer to bring over a movie you've been wanting to see. Encourage him or her to participate in activities that you've enjoyed together in the past, but don't push too hard on this. He or she may feel unable to participate; pushing him or her could just worsen the situation.

Finally, don't be afraid to ask what your friend would like for you to do. Maybe he or she just needs somebody to walk to school with, because he or she feels uncomfortable going in alone. Maybe he or she would like you to be there when he or she approaches a parent about how he or she has been feeling lately and asks for help. Support comes in different forms, some requiring more physical presence than others.

HELPING AN ADULT COPE WITH A STRESS PROBLEM

The discussion in this chapter so far has been about helping someone your own age, or close to your own age, with a stress problem. What happens, though, if you know an adult who's having a difficult time coping with stress and problems resulting from it?

As you know, stress can affect everyone. Even babies and little kids can be affected by stress. It's a sure thing that teens are, and adults are no exception. In fact, it's a rare adult who isn't feeling stressed out in way or another. So, while it would be unusual for an adult to approach a teenager and ask the teen for help, you just might find yourself in a situation in which you have frequent contact with an adult experiencing stress-related problems.

If the affected adult is your mom or dad, or another adult who lives in your home, you'll need to remember that what's going on with one person within a home generally affects the rest of the people living there, as well. If your mom is big-time stressed out, chances are that everyone else in the house will somehow be affected. Your mom might be irritable, or yell at you, or ignore tasks she usually performs. You might come home and find there's nothing to eat for dinner because she was too stressed out to go to the grocery store and cook a meal.

It might be that your dad doesn't understand what's going on with your mom, and is reacting with frustration or anger, advising your mom to "just snap out of it" or "pull yourself together." And, while there's probably nothing that your mom would like to be able to do more, it simply may not be possible for her to overcome her problems and get back to normal on her own.

Watching a parent or other adult struggle with a stress related problem can be disturbing and frustrating, and sometimes even scary. As a teenager, you're aware that adults experience problems on a regular basis. Their problems are different from some of those that affect teens, and adults generally encounter problems that most teenagers haven't had to deal with yet. While you understand that, you might somehow have the expectation that adults should be able to control their problems and not let them affect their lives—or the lives of others who depend on them.

Because the problems of an adult in your house are likely to affect the entire family in a negative manner, it's important that you let someone know how you're feeling. This should not be done in a confrontational or accusatory manner; you shouldn't say something like "You're making everyone in this house miserable" or "I can't stand the way you've been acting lately." Instead, say something like "I've been worried about you lately, and I wonder if there's anything you want to talk about or anything I can do to help you."

That sort of language lets the adult know that you care and want to help. Then you can explain to your mom or other adult that her behavior is affecting your life, and, if applicable, the lives of your siblings, and that you're concerned about what might happen.

You should be aware that people sometimes react differently when they're upset or struggling than they would under normal circumstances. If your mother responds to your overture by getting angry or telling you to leave her alone, try to remember that it's the problem that's causing her to do this—it doesn't mean that she doesn't love you.

If you don't get any satisfaction or resolution from trying to talk to your parent, you'll need to find another trusted adult to confide in. If there's not another parent available to consult, maybe you could talk to a grandparent, aunt, or your mother's best friend, who, in turn, could talk to your mom. If there's no relative you can talk to, perhaps you could ask the advice of a religious leader or someone at your school.

It's very important, however, that you understand that you're not the cause of your mother's problems. The situation, whatever it is, is not your fault, and it's not up to you to fix it. All you can do is express your concern and suggest that your parent seek some help so that she'll feel better.

You can help out at home by picking up some extra chores and being reassuring to younger brothers and sisters, but you're not yet an adult and you shouldn't feel that you have to assume responsibility for the entire household. When all is said and done, it's your parent's responsibility to take care of herself.

TAKING CARE OF YOURSELF WHILE HELPING SOMEONE ELSE

Caregiving is extremely difficult. People who actively care for someone who is sick for a long period of time suffer high rates of depression, often express feelings of being burned out, and sometimes become ill themselves. Even a situation in which you're not providing hands-on care, but are just very concerned about another person, can be demanding, stressful, and wearing. If you're concerned about a friend or family member, keep the following tips in mind:

You can't solve a problem by yourself. As much as you'd like to make someone you care about who's experiencing a problem feel better, you can't do it all by yourself. The other person must play an active role, as well, and, in many cases additional help will be required. Don't beat yourself up if the person you're trying to help doesn't seem to respond as quickly as you'd like. Chances are, he or she appreciates your caring and is glad for your efforts.

Don't be afraid to ask for help. If you're feeling overwhelmed or frustrated, ask someone else for advice or help. It's not a sign of weakness to express to someone that you're concerned about a situation and not sure how to handle it. In fact, seeking help in a difficult situation is a sign of being mature and responsible.

Take time for yourself. Even when you're very worried or concerned about a friend or family member, you've got to take time for yourself and remove yourself from the situation sometimes. If you're helping a friend through a bad time, don't do so at the expense of your other friendships and activities. If you're helping an adult family member, remember that you're still a teenager and you need to have some time to be with friends and enjoy life. Don't let anyone make you feel guilty for wanting down time or understanding that you need to take care of yourself.

Remember to pay attention to how much sleep you get, make sure to eat well, and take time off for fun and relaxation.

WHAT YOU NEED TO KNOW

- ▸ The most important thing you can do for a friend or relative suffering from stress-related problems is to steer him or her toward help.
- ▸ If the person you're trying to help rejects your offer or becomes angry with you, you may have to seek assistance from a trusted adult who can address the situation.
- ▸ Emotional support is letting someone know that you care about him or her and can be very comforting and helpful.
- ▸ Good listening skills are important when you're trying to help someone who has a problem of any kind, including one that's caused by stress.
- ▸ Being physically present can help your friend to feel secure and cared for.
- ▸ Adults are also affected by stress-related problems and might also need your help, but you need to remember that

you're not responsible for the problem and can't fix it by yourself.

➤ When caring for others, it's extremely important to take care of yourself by getting enough sleep, eating well, and making time for some fun and relaxation.

11

Paying for Care

If you've paid attention to national news at all lately, you've probably heard or read about the call for health-care reform. Many people are experiencing difficulty accessing the care they need, even if they have private insurance from an employer or other source. Nearly across the board, employers are asking workers to contribute more toward their health care, forcing many people to rethink their care, and possibly even put off care that they need.

The National Coalition on Health Care, a nonprofit, nonpartisan group of more than 70 organizations working together for better health care for all Americans, reported that employees who are covered by health insurance through their jobs are paying 120 percent more toward copays and deductibles than they were in 2000. The cost to an employer for a single health plan for a family of four averaged $12,700 in 2008. That means that the average health plan costs for a small company with 20 employees would be more than a quarter of a million dollars each year. To offset their costs, employers are asking workers to contribute more and more toward their insurance. The average cost to employees in 2008 was $3,400.

These rapid and significant increases in the cost of health care are squeezing the budgets of employers and individuals, but, hopefully, health-care reform will soon be under way, and services will become more available and equitable. If you are covered by a parent's insurance and can get all the care that you need, consider yourself lucky, because many people do not have that advantage.

Locating and getting access to help for stress-related problems can be particularly challenging, because the problems can be physical, psychological, or both. As you know, exposure to long-term stress can lead to problems ranging from anxiety and depression to colitis, asthma, and sleep disorders. A doctor treating a patient for a stress-related medical problem—migraines, for instance—might recognize that stress is an underlying cause for the condition and recommend that the patient consult with a psychologist or psychiatrist. While your insurance might pay for you to see a doctor about your frequent headaches, it may not provide coverage, or may provide only limited coverage, for psychotherapy.

Another problem is that, while an insurance company normally will cover costs associated with a serious health event, such as a heart attack (which, as you know, can be stress-related), it often is reluctant to cover costs of preventative measures, such as a gym membership, yoga classes, lifestyle assessment, or counseling. It's ironic that trying to find treatment for stress-related disorders can turn out to be so stressful!

Gaining access to mental health care can be especially challenging. Many health-care plans include very limited coverage for counseling or psychotherapy, forcing families to make up the difference between what their insurance covers and the cost of treatment. Psychotherapy fees can cost upward of $75 for a 45-minute session, making the cost prohibitive to many families and individuals.

Hopefully, this situation will improve beginning in January 2010, thanks to a law enacted by former president George W. Bush in 2008. The mental health parity law requires group health plans to provide the same coverage for mental health conditions such as depression, substance abuse, and bipolar disorder as they would for conditions such as heart disease or cancer.

This law won't benefit everyone, however, as it doesn't apply to companies with fewer than 50 employees or to people who buy their own insurance. Still, it will benefit some and may help to raise awareness of issues associated with mental health and its treatment. Mental health advocates worked hard to get the law put into effect, and it's considered a victory in the fight to get treatment for mental health on par with that for physical health.

With more than 45 million Americans uninsured, unemployment on the rise, and the number of employer-provided health plans declining, an increasing number of Americans are relying on publicly funded care, or simply not getting the care that they should.

Health-care plans for children are available, meaning that no child should be left without care, but the applications can be complicated and too difficult for many people to complete. Experts and groups such as the National Coalition on Health Care are working to figure out how to solve these problems as they anticipate an increasing need for health-care services, particularly in the area of mental heath.

UNDERSTANDING DIFFERENT TYPES OF HEALTH-CARE COVERAGE

If you're like most teenagers, you probably don't spend a lot of time thinking about health insurance. It simply isn't a topic that's high on your radar. If you find yourself in a situation where you feel you need treatment that your insurance doesn't cover and your family can't afford to pay for it, however, it may suddenly become an important issue. Let's take a look at the major programs and types of insurances available.

Employment-based health insurance. This is health insurance that an employer provides as a benefit to employees, and sometimes, but not always, their families. The insurance may be provided at no cost to employees, although that is becoming increasingly unusual. Most companies require workers to share some of the costs in the form of copays or deductibles, with requirements varying tremendously from company to company. And it's important to understand that not all companies offer insurance to employees. In Delaware, for instance, 64.2 percent of all companies provide some level of health-insurance overage for employees, according to the Centers for Disease Control and Prevention. In Montana, however, only 40 percent of all companies offer insurance as a benefit to employees. Larger companies are far more likely to provide insurance than smaller ones, and coverage may vary tremendously under this broad umbrella of insurance, depending on the type of policy.

Insurance from one company might come in the form of a Health Maintenance Organization (HMO), for instance, which is a type of health-care coverage that offers care from doctors, hospitals, and other providers with whom the organization has contracted for services. An HMO generally requires approval for many treatments that would automatically be covered with another type of plan, such as a Preferred Provider Organization (PPO) or a Point of Service (POS). HMOs only cover care provided by approved health-care providers who participate in the HMO's plan and agree to its guidelines and restrictions. PPOs are managed care organizations that use hospitals, doctors, and other providers who agree with an insurer to provide care at lower costs to the insurer's clients. PPOs generally are more flexible than HMOs, and usually allow you to choose which health-care providers you wish to use. POSs are sort of combinations of HMOs and PPOs. POSs allow you to see any provider you want, but you'll pay more out of pocket if the provider isn't part of the insurer's network.

Privately purchased health insurance. If someone does not have a job or works for a company that doesn't provide health insurance, or is self-employed, he may need to purchase his own insurance. Who gets insurance and how much he'll have to pay for it varies from state to state. Insurance costs much more in some states than in others, because each state has its own regulations regarding insurance costs. Regulations regarding who can get insurance also vary. In most states, for instance, an applicant can be turned down for insurance based on his health status.

Government-provided health-care coverage. People who don't have jobs that provide health insurance and can't afford to buy their own may qualify for Medicaid or the State Children's Health Insurance Program (SCHIP), which covers anyone who qualifies up to age 18. In 2007, 83 million people were covered by government programs, including 23 million children. Still, more than 8 million children remained without health insurance, according to government statistics.

If your family is a low-income one and doesn't have any health insurance, you might qualify for government-provided health-care coverage. Medicaid is a federal program, but it's state-administered, which means that requirements for eligibility vary from state to state. A big problem occurs when a family's income is too high to qualify for Medicaid, but they don't have enough money to cover medical expenses. You can learn more about who is eligible for Medicaid at www.cms.hhs.gov/medicaid/eligibility or www.cms.hhs.gov/whoiseligible.asp. More information about the SCHIP programs is available at www.cms.hhs.gov/schip or www.insurekidsnow.gov. You also can learn more by calling 1-877-KIDS NOW.

If you are 18 or younger and do not have health insurance, you should know that you often have the right to coverage. Children can be covered by Medicaid in some states; in families where parents don't qualify for Medicaid but can't afford to buy health insurance, children should be covered by SCHIP.

No matter what type of insurance you have, or how it's provided, it's important to read the terms and applications carefully to see what might be covered and what isn't. Also, try to determine the terms of payment for services. Most doctors will submit a request for payment to your insurance companies, but some plans require that you make the payment to the doctor and then submit a claim the insurance company for reimbursement. If you must wait for reimbursement, be sure to make arrangements for payment with the doctor's staff.

DIFFERENT TYPES OF MEDICAL CARE FACILITIES

Medical care is provided in different types of facilities, including doctors' offices, health clinics or community health centers, and hospitals. Doctors in private practices normally expect payment from patients at the time that services are provided, or they bill their patients' insurers for payment. If the services doctors provide are not covered by insurance, doctors may be, understandably, reluctant to perform them. Since many mental health services are still not

The Varying Costs of Professional Services

If paying for mental health care is a concern, remember that different types of professionals charge varying fees for care. Typically, psychiatrists' fees are the highest, while pastoral or community counselors charge the least. Counselors in private practice may be willing to work with you by reducing fees, especially with the current difficult economic conditions.

Where to Look for Mental Health Treatment

If you think you'd benefit from treatment by a mental health professional, don't overlook services offered through community mental health centers or your county's mental health department. Even your school might be able to identify local agencies that can provide affordable treatment and necessary services. Get out your phone book or look online to see what's available, making sure to check out "government services" or "community services."

covered by insurance, counseling or psychotherapy services can be particularly affected.

If your family can't afford to go to a doctor in a private practice because of insurance or financial concerns, there are some options from which you might receive care.

Clinics and community care centers provide treatment for those who can't afford to pay a private-practice doctor. Some clinics are run by hospitals, while others are sponsored by cities and/or funded largely by the federal government. Often, patients who don't have insurance are billed on a sliding scale, depending on their income and the size of their families. No one who needs medical care is turned away, even if they have no income or insurance.

Health Resources and Services Administration (HRSA)–funded Community Health Centers are another option for free or reduced-cost health care for people who are uninsured or underinsured. Some of the centers focus on specific populations, such as migrant workers, Native Americans, people who live in public housing, or those who are homeless. The centers offer both primary and preventative care.

The centers vary greatly in their scope and services, but typically are well run and quite successful. Organized by community-based, usually not-for-profit, health organizations and funded by grants from HRSA, there are thousands of these centers throughout the country, both in urban and rural areas that are considered "medically underserved." That means that there aren't enough private doctors and health-care providers in these areas to care for the nearby population—not necessarily that the areas are poor. Many of these centers, however, are located in low-income areas. Typically, people who work at these Community Health Centers are very dedicated to the health of the local population and do a great job at providing high-quality care, particularly preventive care, even if the health center itself is not luxurious.

If you need to find low-cost or no-cost health care, you or your parents can check with the federal bureau of the HRSA, which maintains a nationwide directory of clinics. More information about the HRSA is available on its Web site at www.ask.hrsa.gov/pc. By typing in your state, city, and zip code and the type of facility in which you're interested, you'll be given a list of clinics in your neighborhood. Or, go to your city's Web site or search for clinics in the city or area in which you live. Another great source for locating free and low cost clinics is NeedyMeds.org, which maintains a state-by-state listing of 3,689 facilities.

HRSA also provides a list of Hill Burton–obligated hospitals and other health-care facilities; because in the past these facilities received government grants and loans for construction and modernization, they are required to provide a certain amount of free and low-cost health care. You can find these facilities on the HRSA Web site, or call the Hill-Burton hotline at 1-800-638-0742.

PAYING FOR MEDICATIONS

If your doctor prescribes a medication for a stress-related condition, either physical or psychological, and you can't afford to buy the medicine, you have several options.

Remember that while medications can be helpful for stress-related conditions, they don't work unless they're used properly and in conjunction with behavioral treatment. Medications work best when combined with treatment, so don't rely on drugs alone.

You or your parents can ask your doctor for free medication samples. Most doctors are happy to provide samples if they have them. A more long-term solution, though, is to apply for free medications from the pharmaceutical companies that manufacture them.

Most drug companies offer these to patients who can't afford them through a variety of assistance programs. Your parents may have to fill out some paperwork and provide proof of financial need in order to qualify, and your doctor will usually need to send a note on your behalf.

You can find out more about free drug programs on the Web sites of the pharmaceutical companies that make the drugs you need. If you were diagnosed with depression and your doctor prescribed Zoloft, for instance, you would go the Web site of Pfizer, Inc., which manufactures that drug.

Some Web sites where you can learn more about obtaining reduced rate or free prescription drugs include:

- Partnership for Prescription Assistance: www.pparx.org
- NeedyMeds program: www.needymeds.org
- Prescription Drug Assistance Programs: www.phrma.org
- RxOutreach: www.rxassist.org

WHAT YOU NEED TO KNOW

- Paying for health care is a problem for an increasing number of Americans who are struggling with rapidly rising costs and, in many cases, declining insurance coverage.
- Even if your family has a good insurance plan, treatment for mental health services are likely not to be covered, or to be minimally covered.
- Health insurance can be provided by an employer, purchased privately, or government run. Plans vary tremendously in what they cover and who is eligible for them.
- If you can't afford medical treatment from a physician in a private practice, check to see if there are any free or reduced-fee health clinics or community health centers available in your area.
- You may be eligible for free medications if they are prescribed to you and you can't afford them.

APPENDIX

Associations and Resources Related to Stress

American Academy for Child and Adolescent Psychiatry
http://www.aacap.org
*The American Academy for Child and Adolescent Psychiatry
supports treatment of disorders in children and adolescents.
There are more than 7,000 child and teenage psychiatrists in
the organization, all dedicated to researching, evaluating, and
diagnosing psychiatric disorders in children and adolescents, as
well as helping their families. The American Academy for Child
and Adolescent Psychiatry's Web site provides information to
encourage understanding about psychiatric disorders in children
and adolescents.*

American Academy of Pediatrics
http://www.aap.org
*The American Academy of Pediatrics is the professional
organization of 60,000 pediatricians in support of psychical,
mental and social health for children from infancy through
adolescence and young adulthood. The American Academy of
Pediatrics Web site contains information on many topics related
to children's health, including an alphabetical database. Users
can also access advice and guidelines about specific health
concerns.*

American Association of Suicidology
http://www.suicidology.org
*Founded in 1968, the American Association of Suicidology (AAS)
supports research and public awareness, education, and training
for both professionals and volunteers. A national clearinghouse
for information on suicide, AAS welcomes individuals as well as
organizational members.*

American Group Psychotherapy Association
http://www.agpa.org
Founded in 1942, the American Group Psychotherapy Association is comprised of psychiatrists who support group therapy as a method to treat a variety of psychotherapy disorders. The American Group Psychotherapy Association offers psychological assistance, arts therapy, psychiatry, alcohol-dependency and marriage counseling, as well as family therapy.

American Foundation for Suicide Prevention
http://www.afsp.org
The American Foundation for Suicide Prevention is committed to research, prevention, and education on suicide. The American Foundation for Suicide Prevention also offers support groups for suicide survivors and information specific to mental health professionals, physicians, as well as the general public. The American Foundation for Suicide Prevention's Web site provides information about depression and suicide, including recognition, treatment, and methods by which to communicate the magnitude of suicide to the public.

American Institute of Stress
http://www.stress.org
Since 1978, the American Institute of Stress has been dedicated to the management and treatment of stress. The American Institute of Stress promotes a healthy lifestyle based on overall well-being. The Web site provides information on the causes, forms, and treatments of stress and stress-related disorders. Methods to combat stress, treatment groups and health professionals are all included on the Web site.

American Medical Association
http://www.ama-assn.org
Found in 1844, the American Medical Association is an organization of doctors and medical professionals dedicated to improving health care, medicine, and public health. The American Medical Association's Web site has information about illnesses, wellness, and public health concerns, as well as a database of doctors and health-care facilities throughout the country.

American Psychiatric Association
http://www.psych.org

The American Psychiatric Association (APA) is a professional
  medical organization with 38,000 members in the United States.
  The American Psychiatric Association is dedicated to providing
  care to those with mental disorders, and to psychiatric education
  as a means to improve overall health.

American Psychological Association

http://www.apa.org

The American Psychological Association (APA) is the world's
  largest association of psychologists. The 150,000 members
  of the American Psychological Association advocate for the
  advancement of psychological knowledge and the use of
  psychology to improve people's lives. A resource for psychologists
  and patients, the American Psychological Association online
  includes information on applying psychology to improve health
  and well-being.

Anxiety Disorders Association of America

http://www.adaa.org

The Anxiety Disorders Association of America is dedicated
  to preventing, treating, and curing anxiety disorders. The
  organization strives to improve the lives of individuals who
  suffer from anxiety disorders. The Anxiety Disorders Association
  of America Web site has statistics and facts about a variety
  of anxiety and stress disorders, as well as resources specific to
  children and teens, including directories of support groups and
  therapists.

Centers for Disease Control and Prevention

http://www.cdc.gov

The Centers for Disease Control and Prevention is run by the U.S.
  Department of Health and Human Services with a focus on
  preventing the spread of disease. While the agency's primary
  function is disease control, its Web site includes a variety of health
  and safety topics.

Center for Mental Health Services

http://www.samhsa.gov

An agency within the Department of Health and Human
  Services, the Center for Mental Health Services is dedicated
  to focusing attention on mental health and substance abuse
  through programs and funding directed towards improving
  the lives of individuals with mental health or substance abuse

problems. The Substance Abuse and Mental Health Services Administration works with national, state, local, community, and faith-based groups. The Web site provides information about 24-hour crisis hotlines as well as treatment centers throughout the country.

Chemically Dependent Anonymous
http://www.cdaweb.org
Chemically Dependent Anonymous is a 12-step program designed to assist individuals in overcoming drug addiction. Chemically Dependent Anonymous provides a program not specific to any particular substance and addresses the mental, physical, and emotional factors surrounding addiction, with a goal of member sobriety.

Depressed Anonymous
http://www.depressedanon.com
Founded with a goal of providing therapy to individuals suffering from depression, Depressed Anonymous works with the chronically depressed, and those recently treated or being treated for depression. Depressed Anonymous supports families of depressed individuals while providing patients with a support community, information, and resources.

Depression and Bipolar Support Alliance
http://www.dbsalliance.org
The Depression and Bipolar Support Alliance is a patient-directed organization dedicated to the understanding, diagnosis, and treatment of bipolar and depression disorders. The Web site provides a comprehensive listing of symptoms, advice on what to do if diagnosed, and steps toward recovery. Users can also access information for the families of individuals suffering from depression or bipolar disorder.

Directory of Family Help
http://www.focusas.com/Directory.html
The Directory of Family Help is an online database of support groups. The site lists groups that assist those suffering from a wide variety of mental health disorders and related concerns.

Eating Disorders Shared Awareness
http://www.mirror-mirror.org

This online database includes detailed information about the types, causes, and signs of eating disorders and how they affect different demographics. Users will find detailed suggestions about recovery and seeking treatment, including a list of treatment centers.

Freedom From Fear
http://www.freedomfromfear.org
Freedom From Fear advocates on behalf of those affected by anxiety disorders and depression by supporting education, community support, and research designed to improve the lives of those suffering from anxiety and related disorders. Freedom From Fear's Web site provides an online screening program for anxiety and depressive disorders and also offers free health-care consultations and other services.

Free Medicine Foundation
http://www.freemedicinefoundation.com
Founded by volunteers, the Free Medicine Foundation assists qualifying families in covering prescription drug costs, specifically low-income families, families without prescription coverage, and families who have used all of their prescription benefits.

Kids Health
http://www.kidshealth.org
Kids Health is designed to provide information about health and well-being to children and teens. It covers a variety of topics and includes daily and seasonal health tips and goal-tracking mechanisms. Users are also able to submit questions.

Mayo Clinic Foundation for Education and Research
http://www.mayo.edu
The Mayo Clinic is a highly respected national network of clinics, research, and health care. The Foundation for Education and Research includes all the Mayo Clinic schools, graduate schools, and certificate programs as well as the Mayo Clinic's research initiatives and clinical trials.

Mayo Clinic Medical Information
http://www.mayoclinic.com
Mayo Clinic Medical Information is the clinic's online health care database. Users can access health information in over 35

categories, explore their symptoms, learn about medical tests and
procedures and read contributions from over 3,000 Mayo Clinic
health care professionals.

Medicine Research Centers
(662) 513-5231
*Medicine Research Centers assists individuals struggling to cover
the cost of their prescriptions. Qualifying patients do not have
Medicaid, any other state or federal aid or prescription insurance
coverage. Family income must prove that prescriptions would
impose a financial hardship. If these criteria are met, Medicine
Research Centers will ship free medicine to your primary-care
physician.*

Mental Health America
http://www.nmha.org
*Formerly the National Mental Health Association, Mental Health
America is a nonprofit organization dedicated to helping all
Americans improve their mental health for greater wellness and
advocating on behalf of those who suffer from mental illness.
Mental Health America runs a number of programs to assist
individuals with mental health concerns and to educate the public.
Mental Health America's Web site offers advice for finding help
and treatment, as well as local support groups and mental health
professionals.*

Mental Health Research Information
http://www.narsad.org
*Previously known as the National Alliance for Research on
Schizophrenia and Depression, the Mental Health Research
Information funds research for a variety of brain and behavior
disorders. The Mental Health Research Information's Web site
includes reliable information on brain and behavior disorders
including, but not limited to, depression, bipolar disorder, and
anxiety disorders.*

National Center for PTSD
http://www.ncptsd.va.gov
*A division of the Department of Veterans Affairs, the National
Center for Post Traumatic Stress Disorder was created to assist
veterans suffering from service-connected post-traumatics stress
disorder. The National Center for Post-Traumatic Stress Disorder*

addresses the affects, diagnosis, and treatment of post-traumatic stress disorder and other stress disorders as they pertain to veterans.

National Clearinghouse for Alcohol and Drug Information
http://ncadi.samhsa.gov
The National Clearinghouse for Alcohol and Drug Information is the largest resource of information regarding alcohol and drug abuse. The Web site includes information on alcohol and drug abuse prevention, intervention, and treatment and also offers a variety of free services.

National Eating Disorders Association
http://www.nationaleatingdisorders.org
The National Eating Disorders Association is a nonprofit organization that provides support to people with eating disorders and their families. The National Eating Disorders Association's Web site provides information and resources about eating disorders for men and women of all ages. Users can access an online toolkit of information on how to help a loved one suffering from or recovering from an eating disorder, as well as search for local treatment options and support groups.

National Institutes of Health
http://www.nih.gov
The National Institutes of Health (NIH) is run by the Department of Health and Human Services and functions as the government's primary institution for medical research. The National Institutes of Health provides medical researchers with billions of dollars in grants, and is dedicated to finding ways to prevent, treat, and cure diseases. The National Institutes of Health Web site offers a comprehensive "A to Z" of health topics.

National Institute of Mental Health
http://www.nimh.nih.gov
A division of the National Institutes of Health, the National Institute of Mental Health is specifically interested in mental illness. The National Institute of Mental Health supports the treatment and prevention of mental illness, and the Web site includes information on each of the mental health topics supported by National Institute of Mental Health research.

NIMH Mood and Anxiety Disorder Program
http://intramural.nimh.nih.gov/mood

Run by the National Institute of Mental Health, the Mood and Anxiety Disorders Program is specific to mood and anxiety problems. It focuses on the diagnosis, treatment, and prevention of these disorders. Disorders of specialty include, but are not limited to, depression, bipolar disorder, obsessive compulsive disorder, post-traumatic stress disorder, and a variety of anxiety disorders. The National Institutes of Health Mood and Anxiety Disorder program has a Web site that features information on a variety of mood and anxiety disorders.

National Registry of Certified Group Psychotherapists
http://www.agpa.org

The National Registry of Certified Group Psychotherapists is comprised of certified group psychotherapists subject to nationally accepted criteria. The National Registry of Certified Group Psychotherapists features mental health professionals, insurance affiliates, education officials, and patients. The organization is dedicated to the quality and care of those suffering from mental disorders.

Overeaters Anonymous
http://www.oa.org

Overeaters Anonymous is a 12-step program designed to support recovery from compulsive overeating. Meetings that protect anonymity foster fellowship between members. Overeaters Anonymous does not focus only on weight loss or diets; it also addresses physical, emotional, and spiritual well-being. To effectively address weight loss, Overeaters Anonymous does not promote a particular diet, but rather encourages each individual to develop an eating plan with a health-care professional and a group sponsor.

Panic Anxiety Disorder Association
http://www.panicanxietydisorder.org

The Panic Anxiety Disorder Association supports individuals with panic and other anxiety disorders. Within the organization is a committee of people recovering from anxiety disorders as well as individuals trained to provide support. The Panic Anxiety Disorder Association supports knowledge and awareness about panic and anxiety disorders. The Web site provides information and resources about anxiety disorders and support networks.

Prescription Drug Abuse
http://www.prescription-drug-abuse.org
Prescription Drug Abuse is an online organization dedicated to treating prescription drug abuse. The Web site offers a free confidential assessment of habitual prescription drug abuse, and will evaluate the assessment and provide users with free treatment referrals. The Web site also contains information about a variety of treatment centers.

Prescription Drug Assistance Program
http://www.phrma.org
The Prescription Drug Assistance Program provides a directory of patient assistance programs by specific medication. Qualifying patients receive their medications at no cost.

Post Traumatic Stress Disorder Gateway
www.ptsdinfo.org
The Post Traumatic Stress Disorder Gateway provides a list of Web sites dealing with the diagnosis and treatment of post-traumatic stress disorder and other stress disorders.

Recovery, Inc.
(312) 337-5661
Recovery, Inc. was founded in 1937 and was based on the work of Dr. Abraham A. Low. The organization is a self help–based mental health program. A nonprofit organization, Recovery, Inc. is entirely managed by its members. The group facilitates local affiliates that meet weekly throughout the United States and the world.

Self Help Group Sourcebook Online
http://mentalhelp.net/selfhelp
The Self Help Group Sourcebook Online provides users with information about more than 1,100 national, international and demonstrational models of self-help support groups, including ideas for starting groups, and communication with existing groups. The Web site provides an extensive database of information from the American Self Help Clearinghouse.

SIDRAN: Sidran Traumatic Stress Foundation
http://www.sidran.org
Sidran supports education, research, and community advocacy regarding traumatic stress and trauma-related disorders.

The Sidran Traumatic Stress Foundation's Web site features publications and information about traumatic stress disorders as well as assessment and research tools.

SMART Recovery
http://www.smartrecovery.org
SMART Recovery provides support groups to individuals in recovery from a variety of addictive behaviors including alcohol abuse, alcoholism, drug and substance abuse, and gambling addiction, among other substances and behaviors. Meetings are held around the country as well as online. Also available online is the SMART Recovery message board, where participants can learn about recovery programs and find support from others.

Stress, Anxiety and Depression Resource Center
http://www.stress-anxiety-depression.org
The Stress, Anxiety and Depression Resource Center provides an online database of information on stress, anxiety disorders, and depression, including resources for treatment.

Students Against Destructive Decisions
http://www.sadd.org
Originally founded as Students Against Drunk Driving, Students Against Destructive Decisions (SADD) is a nonprofit organization dedicated to using peer programs and assistance to prevent underage drinking, substance abuse, violence, depression, and suicide. The Web site contains information about drugs and alcohol abuse, as well as other topics, and contains links to the Students Against Destructive Decisions chapters in all fifty states.

Suicide Prevention Action Network
http://www.spanusa.org
Founded by parents who lost their daughter to suicide in 1996, the Suicide Prevention Action Network strives to prevent suicide through public education and action. The Suicide Prevention Action Network supports public policy aimed at suicide prevention, increased public awareness, and the creation, advancement, and implementation of a national plan to address and combat suicide.

Yellow Ribbon International
http://www.yellowribbon.org
Yellow ribbon is a public health–focused nonprofit dedicated to suicide prevention, specifically among teenagers. Yellow Ribbon works in communities to empower and educate teenagers, as well as their parents and other community members, about suicide. The Web site offers support for survivors, crisis assistance, health-care professionals for long-term treatment, and other resources.

GLOSSARY

adrenaline   A hormone released during times of stress that increases blood pressure and blood sugar levels and makes your heart beat faster, preparing you for the fight-or-flight response.

autoimmune disorders   Problems that occur when something in the immune system goes haywire, causing it to attack a part of the body as if it were an invader looking to cause harm.

automatic thought   The first thought that comes into your mind in response to a specific situation.

bad stress   The type of stress that is acute and occurs over a long period of time.

biological stress   Stress that occurs in response to a biological cause, such as injury or illness.

blended family   A social unit of two previously married parents and their children from their previous and current marriages.

cardiac catheterization   A procedure in which a thin tube is inserted into an artery in the groin or arm and threaded up to reach the coronary arteries, allowing a doctor to check the insides of coronary arteries to determine blockage and other factors affecting the arteries and the heart.

chest X-ray   A test that provides an image of the inside of the chest, including the heart.

cholesterol   A type of fat that can accumulate in the body and is linked to cardiovascular disease.

congenital heart disease   The most common type of major birth defect.

core belief   A deep belief about yourself, usually resulting from what you've heard and experienced in your life.

coronary heart disease   The most common type of heart disease, which occurs when the arteries that allow blood to flow to and from the heart get narrowed and hardened due to buildup of plaque.

cognitive-behavioral therapy   A form of psychotherapy in which therapists help their clients to better manage problems by helping them to change the way they think, behave, and respond to various situations.

congestive heart failure Also known as chronic heart failure, a condition that occurs when the heart can't pump enough blood and oxygen to keep other body organs healthy and functioning properly.

coronary angiography A procedure in which dye is injected through the catheter used in a cardiac catheterization, allowing a doctor to get a better look at the flow of blood and see if blockages are present.

cortisol Known as the stress hormone, a hormone that is released during times of stress and helps the body metabolize glucose, regulate blood pressure, maintain blood sugar levels, boost immune function, respond to inflammation, maintain its internal balance, and regulate fluid and electrolyte levels.

depression An illness characterized by hopelessness and negative perceptions of oneself and of the world. Depression involves the body, mood, and thoughts, and affects the way a person eats and sleeps, the way one feels about oneself, and the way one thinks about things.

diabetes A disorder of metabolism, which is the way our bodies use digested food for growth and energy. Types of diabetes are type 1, which is an autoimmune disease and not related to obesity; type 2, which is the most prevalent type among adults and is associated with obesity; and gestational diabetes, which occurs only in pregnant women.

echocardiogram A medical test that provides an image of the heart.

electrocardiogram (EKG) A medical test that measures the electrical rhythms, rate, and regularity of the heartbeat.

emotional eating Eating that occurs in response to an emotion, such as sadness, anger, happiness, or boredom, rather than in response to actual hunger.

empathy The ability to understand what someone else is feeling, thinking, or experiencing.

employment based health insurance Health insurance that is provided as a benefit to an employee and, often, to his or her family.

endocrine system A set of glands that produce hormones that enter the bloodstream and are transported throughout the body to control functions such as growth, metabolism, and sexual development.

environmental stress Stress that occurs in response to events that occur around us, such as difficult tests, problems with friends, unhappy home situations, or schedules that are too busy.

exercise stress test   A test that measures how effectively the heart pumps when it's working harder than usual, requiring more oxygen for the heart muscle.

fight-or-flight response   A response to stress that prepares your body to address a potentially harmful situation by either standing your ground and dealing with it or running away to escape it.

generation gap   Differences between one age group and another which often result in misunderstandings between generations.

glucocoticoids (GCs)   Hormones and chemicals that help you deal with stressful situations in which you need to think and react quickly by telling the brain to rev up and get prepared.

good stress   The type of stress that puts your body and brain on alert and allows you to respond to situations that require action.

government-provided health care   Health care supported by government programs for people who can not afford their own insurance and meet other requirements.

Health Maintenance Organization (HMO)   A type of insurance plan which covers care provided by approved health-care providers who participate in the HMO's plan and agree to its guidelines and restrictions.

Health Resources and Services Administration (HRSA)–funded Community Health Centers   A facility that provides free or reduced cost health care. The centers are organized by community-based, usually not-for-profit, health organizations and funded by grants from HRSA. There are thousands of these centers throughout the country.

heart disease   A number of conditions that affect the heart, including coronary heart disease and heart attack, congestive heart failure, and congenital heart disease.

hemorrhagic stroke   A stroke that occurs when a blood vessel in the brain breaks or ruptures and blood seeps into brain tissue and causes damage to the brain cells.

Holmes and Rahe stress scale   A listing of life events that result in great stress, used to predict whether people are likely to suffer stress-related problems.

hyperhidrosis   A condition that causes excessive sweating.

hypertension   Also known as high blood pressure, hypertension is a condition that causes the heart to work harder to pump blood to the body and contributes to cardiovascular disease, stroke, eye problems, and kidney disease.

hypothalamus A small part of your brain that sends out an alarm in times of stress, preparing your body for the fight-or-flight response.

immune system A collection of cells, proteins, tissues, and organs that work together to fight off substances that threaten to harm the human body.

immunodeficiency disorder A condition that occurs when parts of the immune system either are not working the way they should or don't exist.

insulin A hormone secreted by the pancreas, an organ located behind the stomach, which regulates the use of sugar in the body.

ischemic stroke A stroke that occurs because either a blood clot or too much plaque clogs blood vessels and blocks the flow of blood to the brain.

journaling The process of using paper and pen or a computer to record how you feel and think about what's happening in your life.

licensed professional counselor A type of mental health professional who holds at least a master's degree in counseling or a related field, has successfully completed supervised clinical experience, and is certified by the state in which he or she will practice.

long-term stress A harmful type of stress that occurs over time on a constant basis.

Medicaid A federal program that provides health-care coverage to people who meet its qualifications. Medicaid is administered through each state.

meditate A process intended to clear your mind of clutter and move into a relaxed state of calm.

mental health parity law A law that requires group health plans to provide the same coverage for mental health as they would for physical conditions.

neuropeptide Y (NPY) A molecule that helps in new tissue growth and is released from certain nerve cells during times of stress.

obesity An excess of body fat that is associated with health problems.

pastoral counselor A counselor who has completed both theological and psychological training and addresses problems in terms of religion and spirituality.

peer pressure Influence, either positive or negative, from other people who are about your same age that can serve as a factor in what you wear, who your friends are, how you speak, where you shop, and other aspects of your life.

Point of Service (POS)   A type of health insurance that allows patients to choose any health-care provider they want but charges more out of pocket if the provider is not part of the plan's network.

post-traumatic stress disorder (PTSD)   A disorder triggered by a traumatic event and characterized by recurring flashbacks or nightmares about the event, a need to avoid any reminder of the event, and a constant feeling of dread.

Preferred Provider Organization (PPO)   A type of health insurance that generally is flexible in allowing patients to choose their own health-care providers.

privately purchased health insurance   Health insurance obtained and paid for by an individual or family.

psychiatrist   A medical doctor who specializes in diagnosing and treating mental conditions and is qualified to prescribe medicines.

psychologist   A trained mental health professional who is qualified to diagnose and treat mental, emotional, and behavioral disorders.

psychological stress   Stress that comes from within, usually caused by expectations you set for yourself, or those that are imposed on you by others.

psychotherapist   A person who provides counseling services, either with or without a license, ranging from psychiatrists to ministers.

self-esteem   The quality of liking yourself and who you are.

self injury   The act of intentionally harming oneself by cutting, burning, or another method.

State Children's Health Insurance Program (SCHIP)   A publicly funded insurance program for children up to 18 years of age who are not otherwise covered.

stress   The means by which your body responds to pressure caused by a situation that causes you to adjust and respond. Also can refer to your response to that situation.

stressor   The situation, thought, or event that causes you to feel stressed.

short-term stress   A beneficial type of stress that occurs in response to a particular situation and quickly recedes once the situation has been resolved.

social workers   Someone who is licensed or certified to work with clients in a clinical setting to prevent, diagnose, and treat mental, behavioral, and emotional disorders.

sphygmomanometer   A device consisting of a stethoscope, arm cuff, dial, pump, and valve that is used to measure high blood pressure.

support system   People who you know and trust, and feel you can approach and ask for help when you need it.

READ MORE ABOUT IT

Auerbach, Stephen M., and Sandra E. Grambling. *Stress Management: Psychological Foundations.* Boston: Prentice Hall, 1997.

Aldwin, Carolyn M., and Emmy E. Werner. *Stress, Coping, and Development, Second Edition: An Integrative Perspective.* New York: The Guilford Press, 2007.

American Medical Association. *The American Medical Association Guide to Talking to Your Doctor.* New York: Wiley, 2001.

Blonna, Richard. *Coping with Stress in a Changing World.* New York: McGraw Hill, 2006.

Boss, Pauline. *Family Stress Management.* Thousand Oaks, Calif.: Sage Publications, 2001.

Carlson, Richard. *Don't Sweat the Small Stuff for Teens.* New York: Hyperion, 2000.

Charlesworth, Edward A., and Ronald G. Nathan. *Stress Management: A Comprehensive Guide to Wellness.* New York: Ballantine Books, 2004.

Colbert, Don. *Stress Management 101.* Nashville, Tenn.: Thomas Nelson Publishers, 2006.

Covey, Sean. *Daily Reflections for Highly Effective Teens.* New York: Fireside, 1999.

Crum, Albert. *The 10 Step Method of Stress Relief: Decoding the Meaning and Significance of Stress.* Boca Raton, Fla.: CRC, 2000.

Davidson, Jeff. *The Complete Idiot's Guide to Managing Stress.* New York: Alpha Books, 1999.

Davis, Martha, Elizabeth Robbins Eshelman, Matthew McKay, and Patrick Fanning. *The Relaxation and Stress Reduction Workbook.* Oakland, Calif.: New Harbinger Publications, 2008.

Elkin, Allen. *Stress Management for Dummies.* New York: Wiley, 1999.

Esherick, Joan. *Balancing Act: A Teen's Guide to Managing Stress.* Science of Health: Youth and Well-Being. Broomall, Pa.: Mason Crest Publishers, 2005.

Fox, Annie. *Too Stressed to Think?: A Teen's Guide to Staying Sane When Life Makes You Crazy.* Minneapolis: Free Spirit Publishing, 2005.

146

Ginsburg, Kenneth R., and Martha M. Jablow. *Giving Your Child Roots and Wings.* Elk Grove Village, Ill.: American Academy of Pediatrics, 2006.

Greenberg, Jerrold. *Comprehensive Stress Management.* New York: McGraw Hill, 2008.

Groves, Dawn. *Stress Reduction for Busy People: Finding Peace in an Anxious World.* San Francisco: New World Library, 2004.

Hipp, Earl. *Fighting Invisible Tigers: A Stress Management Guide for Teens.* Minneapolis: Free Spirit Publishing, 2008.

Hyde, Margaret O., and Elizabeth H. Forsyth. *Stress 101: An Overview for Teens.* Teen Overviews. Breckinridge, Colo.: Twenty-First Century Books, 2007.

Jones, Marilee, Kenneth R. Ginsburg, and Martha M. Jablow. *Less Stress, More Success: A New Approach to Guiding Your Teen Through College Admissions and Beyond.* Elk Grove Village, Ill.: American Academy of Pediatrics, 2006.

Kottler, Jeffrey, and David Chen. *Stress Management and Prevention: Applications to Daily Life.* Pacific Grove, Calif.: Brooks Cole, 2007.

Lawton, Sandra Augustyn, ed. *Stress Information for Teens: Health Tips About the Mental and Physical Consequences of Stress.* Teen Health. Detroit: Omnigraphics, 2008.

Lazarus, Judith. *Stress Relief and Relaxation Techniques.* New York: McGraw Hill, 2000.

Lazarus, Richard S. *Stress and Emotion: A New Synthesis.* New York: Springer Publishing Company, 2006.

Leeson, Nick, and Ivan Tyrrell. *Back from the Brink: Coping with Stress.* New York: Virgin Books, 2005.

Leyden-Rubenstein, Lori. *The Stress Management Handbook.* New York: McGraw Hill, 1999.

Loehr, James E., and Mark H. McCormack. *Stress for Success.* New York: Three Rivers Press, 1998.

Lush, Jean, and Pam Vredevelt. *Women and Stress: Practical Ways to Manage Tension.* Ada, Mich.: Revell, 2008.

Mason, John L. *Guide to Stress Reduction.* 2nd ed. Berkeley, Calif.: Celestial Arts, 2004.

McEwen, Bruce. *The End of Stress As We Know It.* Washington, D.C.: Joseph Henry Press, 2002.

Michaels Wheeler, Claire. *10 Simple Solutions to Stress: How to Tame Tension and Start Enjoying Your Life.* Oakland, Calif.: New Harbinger Publications, 2007.

Nathan, Ronald G. *Doctor's Guide to Instant Stress Relief.* New York: Ballantine Books, 1989.

Peques, Deborah Smith. *30 Days to Taming Your Stress.* Eugene, Oreg.: Harvest House, 2007.

Posen, David. *The Little Book of Stress Relief.* Toronto, Ont.: Key Porter Books, 2009.

Powell, Mark. *Stress Relief: The Ultimate Teen Guide.* Lanham, Md.: Scarecrow Press, 2007.

Rice, Phillip L. *Stress and Health.* Florence, Ky.: Wadsworth Publishing, 1998.

Robbins, Paul R. *Coping with Stress: Commonsense Strategies.* Jefferson, N.C.: McFarland & Company, 2007.

Romas, John A., and Manoj Sharma. *Practical Stress Management: A Comprehensive Workbook for Managing Change and Promoting Health.* Boston, Mass.: Benjamin Cummings, 2009.

Seaward, Brian. *Hot Stones and Funny Bones: Teens Helping Teens Cope with Stress and Anger.* Deerfield, Fla.: HCI Teens, 2002.

Selye, Hans. *The Stress of Life.* New York: McGraw Hill, 1978.

Shores, Steve. *Stressbusters: For Teens Under Pressure.* Dewitt, Mich.: Vine Books, 2002.

Smith, Jonathan C. *Stress Management: A Comprehensive Handbook of Techniques and Strategies.* New York: Springer Publishing Companies, 2002.

Snyder, C. R. *Coping with Stress: Effective People and Processes.* New York: Oxford University Press, 2001.

Sutherland, Lucy, and J. P. Cooper. *Strategic Stress Management.* New York: Palgrave Macmillan, 2002.

Swindoll, Charles R. *Stress Relief: Calm Answers for a Hurried Life.* Fullerton, Calif.: Insight for Living, 1995.

Tubesing, Donald A. *Kicking Your Stress Habits: A Do-It-Yourself Guide for Coping with Stress.* Duluth, Minn.: Whole Person Associates, 1981.

Weinstein, Richard. *The Stress Effect.* Avery Health Guides. New York: Avery Trade, 2004.

Weiss, Brian. *Eliminating Stress, Finding Inner Peace.* Carlsbad, Calif.: Hay House, 2003.

Youngs, Bettie B., and Jennifer Youngs. *A Taste-Berry Teen's Guide to Managing the Stress and Pressures of Life.* Deerfield, Fla.: HCI Teens, 2001.

INDEX

A

abuse 10, 15, 24, 64
Academy of Cognitive Therapy 98
Academy of Psychosomatic Medicine
  5
acne 38
addiction 77
adrenal glands 33
adrenaline 33, 68
    overexposure to 54
adults. *See also* parents
    generation gap with teens 21–22
    helping to cope with stress 115–117
    talking to 112, 113
aggression
    causes of 45
    stress and 78–79
AIDS (acquired immunodeficiency
  syndrome) 57
alcohol abuse 76–77
allergic disorders 57–58
American Academy of Pediatrics 5, 6, 50
American Physiological Association 5
anger 44–45
Angie's list 100
angina 55
anorexia nervosa 76
anxiety 42–43
    lack of sleep and 80
    medications used to treat 107
    prevalence among teens 5
anxiety disorders 65–67
Association for Behavioral and
  Cognitive Therapies 98
asthma 53, 58
autoimmune disorders 57
automatic thought 104
    replacing with new thought 105

B

beliefs. *See* core belief

belly pain 5, 37
benzodiazepines 107
biological causes of stress 11–13
blended families 23
blood pressure 53–54
body, response to stress 3–4, 5, 10, 32–35
body image 24–25, 63–64
brain
    long-term exposure to stress and
      62
    response to stress 4, 10, 33, 68
    stroke and 56
breathing, deep 83–84
bulimia nervosa 76
bullying 78
Bush, George W. 121

C

cancer 58–59
Cannon, Walter Bradford 5
car accidents, alcohol-related 77
cardiac catheterization 55
causes of stress. *See* sources of stress
Centers for Disease Control and
    Prevention (CDC) 62
chemotherapy 57
chest pain 5, 55
cholesterol 54
circadian rhythm 80
clinic(s), mental-health 125
clinical psychologists 99
clinical social workers 100
cognitive-behavioral therapy 97–98
    PTSD and 44
    sense of failure and 46
    what to expect during 103–104
communication
    generation gap in 22
    and stress relief 86–87
Community Health Centers 125–126
compulsive spending 77–78

compulsive work/studying 79
confusion 47–48
congenital heart disease 56
congestive heart failure 56
consent-to-treatment 101
control, lack of
    recognizing in stressful situations
        17
    teens and 20–22, 73
core belief 104
    addressing and changing 105–106
coronary angiography 55
coronary heart disease 55
cortisol 33
    and immune system 58
    overexposure to 34, 54
counseling psychologists 99
counselors
    fees of 124
    licensed professional 99
    pastoral 100
cutting, in response to stress 75–76

D

death
    leading cause among teenagers 77
    as source of stress 24
Debtors Anonymous 78
deep breathing 83–84
depression 46–47, 67–70
    causes of 69
    lack of sleep and 80
    medications for 107–108
    prevalence among teens 5
    and sleep problems 81
    symptoms of 69, 113
    treatment for 107
    untreated 113
developmental psychologists 99
diabetes 60–61
disorganization 88
disorientation 47–48
distorted thoughts, learning to
    recognize 87–91
divorce, stress associated with 23–24,
    44–45
drug abuse 76–77

E

eating
    healthy 82
    stress and 59–60, 76

eating disorders 76
echocardiogram 55
eczema 58
electrocardiogram (EKG) 55
emotional responses to stress 41–49
emotional support, providing 113–115
empathy 113–114
endocrine system 10
environment, teens' lack of control over
    20–22, 73
environmental stress 13–14
evolution, and fight-or-flight response
    4, 35
exercise
    benefits of 85
    fitting in daily schedule 90
    moderate 85
    and sleep 81
    vigorous 86
exercise stress test 55
expectations, and stress 14–16, 23,
    24–26, 46, 63, 104

F

failure, sense of 46
family. See also parents
    blended 23
    as source of stress 15, 22–24, 46,
        104
    support by 11
fat growth 60
fear 42–43
    anxiety disorders and 66
    of terrorist attacks 29
fight-or-flight response 4, 33–34
    endocrine system in 10
    evolution and 4, 35
    origins of term 5
financial concerns
    health care 120–127
    and stress 13
food, use for escape 59, 76
food allergies 58
friends. See also peer(s)
    asking for help 96
    helping friends deal with stress
        110–115

G

gambling 77
gastrointestinal problems 5, 37
general adaptation syndrome 5

generalized anxiety disorder (GAD) 66
generation gap 21–22
genetics
    and addiction 77
    and stress 7
Georgetown University Medical Center 60
girls, sources of stress among 14, 24–25,
    63–64
glucocoticoids (GCs) 68

H
Harvard Medical School 5
headaches
    as source of stress 11
    stress and 5, 39, 52
health care. *See also* mental health
    treatment
        free or reduced-cost 125–126
        gaining access to 120–121
        types of facilities 124–126
health insurance
        employment-based 122–123
        government-provided 123–124
        limitations of 98, 121
        mental health parity law and 121
        privately purchased 123
        rising costs of 120
Health Maintenance Organization
    (HMO) 122–123
Health Resources and Services
    Administration (HRSA) 125
heart attack 55
heart disease 54, 55, 56
help. *See also* mental health treatment
    offering to adults 115–117
    offering to friends 110–115
    when to ask for 93–95, 118
    who to ask for 95–97
hemorrhagic stroke 56
high blood pressure 53–54
Hill Burton-obligated hospitals 126
HMO 122–123
Holmes, Thomas 12
Holmes and Rahe stress scale 12, 13,
    51
homeostasis 33
H1N1 (swine flu) 18
hormones, in response to stress 10, 33
hospitals, Hill Burton-obligated 126
HRSA. *See* Health Resources and
    Services Administration
hyperhidrosis 38

hypertension 53–54
hypothalamus 4, 33

I
illness
    and stress 5, 11–13
    stress as cause of 13, 34, 37–39,
        50–61
immune response 57
immune system 38–39, 56–58
immunodeficiency disorder 57
immunosuppressive medicines 57
information. *See also* Internet resources
    in addressing stress 18
    v. experience 22
injury. *See also* self-injury
    as cause of stress 5, 11–13
insulin 60
insurance. *See* health insurance
Internet, and parent-teen stress 22
Internet resources
    for cognitive-behavioral therapy 98
    for endocrine system 11
    for free and low-cost care 123,
        126, 127
    for self-esteem 26
    for stress management 6
irritability, in response to stress 44–45
irritable bowel syndrome 37
ischemic stroke 56

J
job, as source of stress 13
Johns Hopkins University, School of
    Public Health 53
journaling 87
juvenile rheumatoid arthritis 57

K
KidsHealth.org 26

L
leukemia 58
licensed professional counselors 99
life experiences, and stress 7
lifestyle changes
    eating 82
    exercising 85–86
    inability to implement 93–94
    journaling 87
    practical advice for 88–90
    relaxing 82–84

sleeping 81
talking 86–87
listening to others 87, 114
long-term stress 3, 51–52
negative effects of 6, 50–51, 121
physical effects of 37, 52–61
psychological effects of 62–71
lupus 57
lymphoma 58

M

management of stress 17
help with 94–100, 110–119
Internet resources for 6
mantra 85
MAOIs. *See* monoamine oxidase
inhibitors
Medicaid 123, 124
medical care facilities, types of 124–126
medications
immunosuppressive 57
paying for 126–127
for stress-related problems 107–108
meditation techniques 84–85
memory
lack of sleep and 80
stress and 62, 68
mental health professionals 97–100
fees of 124
mental health treatment
consenting to 101
locating and gaining access to
97–100, 121
parents and 101, 102
paying for 120–127
sharing information about 102
what to expect during 102–105
where to look for 125
migraine headaches 11, 39
military personnel, stress experienced
by 10
monoamine oxidase inhibitors (MAOIs)
108
muscle relaxation 84
myocardial infarction 55
My Pyramid 82

N

National Cancer Institutes 58
National Coalition on Health Care 120,
122

National Institute of Mental Health 107
National Sleep Foundation 81
National Suicide Prevention Lifeline 112
neck pain 52
NeedyMeds program 126, 127
Nemours Foundation 11
neuropeptide Y (NPY) 60

O

obesity 59–60, 76
obsessive-compulsive disorder (OCD)
67
om 85
overeating 59–60, 76
overspending 77–78

P

panic attacks 36, 67
parents
asking for help 96
expectations of, and stress on
teens 15, 23, 46, 104
generation gap with teens 21–22
and mental health treatment of
teen 101, 102
Partnership for Prescription Assistance
127
pastoral counselors 100, 124
paying for care 120–127
pediatrician, asking for help 97
peer(s). *See also* friends
expectations of 15–16
positive influence of 27
peer pressure 26–29
forms of 27
plan for dealing with 28–29
perfectionism, and depression 46–47
personality
and core belief 104
and stress 6–7, 9–10, 16
perspiration 36, 38
pharmaceutical companies, free
medications from 127
physical response to stress 3–4, 5, 10,
32–35
physical symptoms, stress-related
52–53
pituitary gland 33
Point of Service (POS) 123
post-traumatic stress disorder (PTSD)
14, 43–44, 66

Preferred Provider Organization (PPO) 123
Prescription Drug Assistance Programs 127
psychiatrists 98–99
    fees of 124
psychological stress 14–16, 41–49, 62–71
    abuse and 64
    new sources of 29–30
    poor self-esteem and 63–64
    unrealistic expectations and 63
    violence and 64–65
psychologists 99
psychotherapists 100
PTSD. *See* post-traumatic stress disorder

Q
quiet time 89

R
Rahe, Richard 12
relatives. *See also* family
    asking for help 96
relaxation 82–84
response to stress
    assessment of 73–74
    emotional 41–49
    information and 18
    physical 3–4, 5, 10, 32–35
    proactive 17
    three levels of 73
    unhealthy 74–79
    variability in 6–7, 9–10, 16
rest, and coping with stress 80
rheumatoid arthritis, juvenile 57
RxOutreach 127

S
safety, stress associated with 14, 29
school, as source of stress 13
school psychologists 99
scleroderma 57
selective serotonin reuptake inhibitors (SSRIs) 107, 108
self-esteem 25–26
    and dealing with peer pressure 28
    poor, and psychological stress 63–64
    sources of information on 26

self-injury, in response to stress 75–76
Selye, Hans 5
sense of failure 46
September 11, 2001, terrorist attacks 29, 47
sexual dysfunction 39
short-term stress 3, 36–39
skin problems
    immunodeficiency disorders and 57
    stress and 38
sleep
    and coping with stress 80
    depression and problems with 81
    patterns among teens 80–81
    stress and problems with 5, 38
    tips for improving 81
social phobia 66
social workers 100
societal expectations, and stress 24–26
sociological causes of stress 13–14
sources of stress 9
    biological 11–13
    environmental/sociological 13–14
    family pressures as 15, 22–24, 46, 104
    lack of control as 20–22, 73
    new 29–30
    peer pressures as 15–16, 26–29
    psychological 14–16
    societal expectations as 24–26
    unrelenting 94
sphygmomanometer 53
SSRIs. *See* selective serotonin reuptake inhibitors
State Children's Health Insurance Program (SCHIP) 123, 124
stomachache 5, 37
stress. *See also* management of stress; response to stress; sources of stress
    bad 3, 7
    biological causes of 11–13
    definition of 2
    emotional response to 41–49
    environmental/sociological causes of 13–14
    fighting back against 79–91
    good 2–3, 7
    helping others deal with 110–119
    impact of 7
    long-term 3, 6, 51–52

long-term physical effects of 37,
52–61
long-term psychological effects of
62–71
personality and 6–7, 9–10, 16
physical response to 3–4, 5, 10,
32–35
prevalence among teens 2, 3, 5,
14
psychological causes of 14–16
short-term 3, 36–39
study of 4–5
symptoms of 72
stressful situations
anticipating and addressing
17–18
avoiding 79
talking over 86–87
stressors
definition of 2
universal 13, 51
variability in response to 6–7,
9–10
stress overload 7
stroke 56
studying, compulsive 79
suicide 70–71
antidepressant drugs and 108
compulsive spending and 78
friends and prevention of 112
among teens 70, 113
support system 95–96
sweating, excessive 36, 38
swine flu (H1N1) 18

T

teacher, asking for help 96
technology, and generation gap 22
teens
daily pressures on 16–17
family pressures on 22–24
generation gap with adults 21–22
lack of control over environment
20–22, 73
leading cause of death among 77

peer pressures on 26–29
risk for stress-related problems
19–20
self-esteem and 25–26
sleep patterns of 80–81
stress among 2, 3, 5, 14
suicide among 70, 113
teeth grinding 52
tension headaches 39
terrorist attacks 29, 47
thought(s)
automatic 104, 105
distorted, learning to recognize
87–91
traumatic experience
and PTSD 43
responses following 62
and stress 10–11
treatment. *See* mental health treatment
tricyclic antidepressants 107

U

University of Michigan in Ann Arbor 2

V

Vietnam War 14
violence, and stress 29, 64–65
vitamin B 82

W

Wansink, Brian 59
war, and PTSD 14
Web sites. *See also* Internet
reliable 6
weight gain 59–60
withdrawal
explanations for 45
stress and 78
work, compulsive 79

X

X-ray, chest 55

Y

youth group leader, asking for help 96